High School Talksheets

Psalms and Proverbs

YOUTH SPECIALTIES TITLES

Professional Resources
The Church and the American Teenager
    (previously released as Growing Up in America)
Developing Spiritual Growth in Junior High Students
Equipped to Serve: Volunteer Youth Worker
    Training Course
Feeding Your Forgotten Soul
Help! I'm a Volunteer Youth Worker!
High School Ministry
How to Recruit and Train Volunteer Youth Workers
    (previously released as Unsung Heroes)
Junior High Ministry (Revised Edition)
The Ministry of Nurture
Organizing Your Youth Ministry
Peer Counseling in Youth Groups
Advanced Peer Counseling in Youth Groups
The Youth Minister's Survival Guide
Youth Ministry Nuts and Bolts

Discussion Starter Resources
Amazing Tension Getters
Get 'Em Talking
High School TalkSheets
Junior High TalkSheets
High School TalkSheets: Psalms and Proverbs
Junior High TalkSheets: Psalms and Proverbs
More High School TalkSheets
More Junior High TalkSheets
Option Plays
Parent Ministry TalkSheets
Tension Getters
Tension Getters Two

Ideas Library
Ideas Combo 1-4, 5-8, 9-12, 13-16, 17-20,
21-24, 25-28, 29-32, 33-36, 37-40, 41-44,
45-48, 49-52, 53, 54
Ideas Index

Youth Ministry Programming
Adventure Games
Creative Bible Lessons
Creative Programming Ideas for Junior High Ministry
Creative Socials and Special Events
Facing Your Future
Good Clean Fun
Good Clean Fun, Volume 2
Great Fundraising Ideas for Youth Groups
Great Games for City Kids
Great Ideas for Small Youth Groups
Great Retreats for Youth Groups
Greatest Skits on Earth
Greatest Skits on Earth, Volume 2
Holiday Ideas for Youth Groups (Revised Edition)
Hot Illustrations for Youth Talks
Hot Talks
Junior High Game Nights
More Junior High Game Nights

On-Site: 40 On-Location Youth Programs
Play It! Great Games for Groups
Play It Again! More Great Games for Groups
Road Trip
Super Sketches for Youth Ministry
Teaching the Bible Creatively
Teaching the Truth About Sex
Up Close and Personal: How to Build Community in
    Your Youth Group

4th-6th Grade Ministry
Attention Grabbers for 4th-6th Graders
4th-6th Grade TalkSheets
Great Games for 4th-6th Graders
How to Survive Middle School
Incredible Stories
More Attention Grabbers for 4th-6th Graders
More Great Games for 4th-6th Graders
Quick and Easy Activities for 4th-6th Graders
More Quick and Easy Activities for 4th-6th Graders
Teach 'Toons

Clip Art
ArtSource Volume 1—Fantastic Activites
ArtSource Volume 2—Borders, Symbols, Holidays and
    Attention Getters
ArtSource Volume 3—Sports
ArtSource Volume 4—Phrases and Verses
ArtSource Volume 5—Amazing Oddities and
    Appalling Images
ArtSource Volume 6—Spiritual Topics
Youth Specialties Clip Art Book
Youth Specialties Clip Art Book, Volume 2

Video
Edge TV
God Views
The Heart of Youth Ministry: A Morning with
    Mike Yaconelli
Next Time I Fall in Love Video Curriculum
Promo Spots for Junior High Game Nights
Resource Seminar Video Series
Understanding Your Teenage Video Curriculum
Witnesses

Student Books
Going the Distance
Grow for It Journal
Grow for It Journal Through the Scriptures
How to Live with Your Parents Without Losing
    Your Mind
I Don't Remember Dropping the Skunk, But I
    Do Remember Trying to Breathe
Next Time I Fall in Love
Next Time I Fall in Love Journal
101 Things to Do During a Dull Sermon

High School Talksheets

Psalms and Proverbs

50 Discussion Starters
from the Scriptures

Rick Bundschuh
and Tom Finley

Youth
Specialties

ZondervanPublishingHouse

Grand Rapids, Michigan
A Division of HarperCollins Publishers

High School TalkSheets Psalms and Proverbs

Copyright©1994 by Youth Specialties, Inc.

Youth Specialties Books, 1224 Greenfield Drive, El Cajon, California 92021, are published by Zondervan Publishing House, 5300 Patterson, S.E., Grand Rapids, Michigan 49530.

Library of Congress Cataloging-in-Publication Data

Bundschuh, Rick, 1951-
    High school talksheets : Psalms and Proverbs : fifty discussion starters
    from the Scriptures / Rick Bundschuh and Tom Finley.
        p. cm.
    ISBN 0-310-49131-2 : $12.95
    1. Bible. O.T. Psalms—Study and teaching. 2. Bible. O.T. Proverbs—Study and teaching. 3. High School
students—Religious life. 4. Church group work with teenagers. I. Finley, Tom, 1951- . II. Title. III. Title: High
School talk sheets.
BS1451.B86 1994
268' .433—dc20

                                                                                        94-16425
                                                                                        CIP

Edited by Noel Becchetti and Janet Miclean
Typography and design by Church Art Works

Printed in the United States of America

96 97 98 99/ MAL /6 5 4 3

High School Talksheets

Psalms and Proverbs

Table of Contents

HOW TO USE TALKSHEETS

You have in your possession a very valuable book. It contains fifty instant discussions for high school youth groups. Inside, you will find reproducible TalkSheets covering a wide variety of hot topics, plus simple step-by-step instructions on how to use them. All you need for fifty thought-provoking meetings is this book and access to a copy machine.

TalkSheets are versatile and easy to use. They can be utilized in a group meeting, a Sunday school class, or during Bible study. They can be used either in small or large groups of people. The discussions they instigate can be as brief as twenty minutes, or as long as interest remains and time allows. You can build an entire youth group meeting around a single TalkSheet, or you can use TalkSheets to supplement other materials and resources you might be using. The possibilities are endless.

TalkSheets are much more than just another type of curriculum or workbook. They invite excitement and involvement in discussing important issues and growth in faith. TalkSheets deal with key topics that young people want to talk about. With interesting activities, challenging questions, and eye-catching graphics, TalkSheets will capture the attention of your audience and will help them think and learn. The more you use TalkSheets, the more your young people will look forward to them.

TALKSHEETS ARE DISCUSSION STARTERS

While TalkSheets can be used as curriculum for your program, they are primarily designed to be used as discussion starters. Everyone knows the value of a good discussion in which young people are interacting with each other. When they are talking about a given subject, they are most likely thinking seriously about it and trying to understand it better. They are formulating and defending their points of view and making decisions and choices. Discussion helps truth rise to the surface, thereby making it easier for young people to discover it for themselves. There is no better way to encourage learning than through discussion.

A common fear among youth group leaders reticent about leading a group of young people in discussion is, "What if the kids in my group just sit there and refuse to participate?" It is because of this fear that many choose to show a movie or give a prepared lecture.

Usually, the reason young people fail to take part in a discussion is simple: They haven't had the time or the opportunity to organize their thoughts. Most high school students haven't yet developed the ability to "think on their feet"—to be able to present their ideas spontaneously and with confidence. They are afraid to speak for fear they might sound stupid.

TalkSheets remove this fear. They offer a chance to interact with the subject matter in an interesting, challenging, and nonthreatening way, *before* the actual discussion begins. Not only does this give them time to organize their thoughts and to write them down, but it also helps remove any anxiety they might feel. Most will actually look forward to sharing their answers and hearing others' responses to the same questions. They will be ready for a lively discussion.

A STEP-BY-STEP USER'S GUIDE

TalkSheets are very easy to use, but do require some preparation on your part. Follow these simple instructions and your TalkSheet discussion will be successful:

1 Choose the right TalkSheet for your group. Each TalkSheet deals with a different topic. The one you choose will have a lot to do with the needs and the maturity level of your group. It is not necessary (or recommended) to use the TalkSheets in the order in which they appear in this book.

2 Try it yourself. Once you have chosen a specific TalkSheet, answer the questions and do the activities yourself. Imagine your students participating. This "role playing" will give you firsthand knowledge of what you will be requiring of your young people. As you fill out the TalkSheet, think of additional questions, activities, and Scriptures.

3 Read the Leader's Instructions (on the back of each TalkSheet). Numerous tips and ideas for getting the most out of your discussion are contained in the Leader's Instructions. Add your own thoughts and ideas. Fill in the date and the name of the group in the top right hand corner of the leader's page.

4 Make enough copies for everyone. Each student will need his or her own copy. This book makes the assumption that everyone has access to a copy machine but any method of duplicating will suffice. Only the student's side of the TalkSheet needs to be copied. The leader's material on the other side is just for you, the leader.

Keep in mind that you are able to make copies for your group because we have given you permission to do so. U.S. copyright laws haven't changed. It is still mandatory that you request permission from a publisher before making copies of other published material. It is illegal not to do so. Permission is given for you to make copies of this material for your group only, not for every youth group in your state. Thank you for your cooperation.

Introduce the topic. In most cases, it is important to introduce, or set up, the topic before you pass out the TalkSheets to your group. Any method will do as long as it is short and to the point. Be careful not to over-introduce the subject. Don't use an introduction that is too "preachy" or which resolves the issue before you get started. You want only to stimulate interest and instigate discussion. That is the primary purpose of the introduction.

The simplest way to introduce the topic is verbally. You can tell a story, share an experience, or describe a conflict having to do with the subject. You might ask a simple question, such as, "What is the first thing you think of when you hear the word _____?" (whatever the topic is). After some have volunteered a few answers, you could reply, "It sounds like we all have different ideas on the subject; let's investigate it a bit further," or something similar. Then you distribute the TalkSheets, make certain everyone has a pen or pencil, and you're on your way.

Here are some ways of introducing any of the topics in this book, all of which, of course, should be pertinent:

1. Show a short film or video.
2. Read an interesting passage from a book or magazine article.
3. Play a popular record dealing with the theme.
4. Present a short skit or dramatic reading.
5. Play a simulation game or role play.
6. Present some current statistics, survey results, or read a recent newspaper article.
7. Use an icebreaker, such as a humorous game. For example, if the topic is "Fun," play a game to begin the discussion. If the topic is "Success," consider a game whose players experience success or failure.
8. Use posters, slides, or any other audio-visual aids available to help concentrate focus.

There are, of course, many other possibilities. The introduction of the topic is left to your discretion and good judgment. You are limited only by your own creativity. Suggestions are offered with each TalkSheet, but they are not mandatory for success. Remember that the introduction is an integral part of each session. It helps set the tone and will influence the kinds of responses you receive. Don't load the introduction to the point that the answer is revealed, and the students feel hesitant about sharing their own opinions.

Give students time to work on their TalkSheet. After you introduce the topic, pass out a copy of the TalkSheet to each member of the group. Members should also have a Bible, as well as writing implements. There are usually five or six activities on each TalkSheet. If time is limited, direct your students' interest to the specific part of the TalkSheet in which you wish them to participate.

Decide whether or not they should complete the TalkSheet on an individual basis or in groups. Encourage your group to consider what the Bible has to say as they complete their TalkSheets.

Announce a time limit for their written work, then make them aware when one or two minutes remain. They may need more time, or less. Use your own judgment, depending upon your observations of the majority of the group. The discussion is now ready to begin.

Lead the discussion. In order for the TalkSheets to be used effectively, all members of your group need to be encouraged to participate. You can foster a climate that is conducive to discussion by communicating that each person's opinion is worthwhile and each has a responsibility to contribute to the rest of the group. A variety of opinions is necessary for these TalkSheets to have meaning.

If your group is large, you may want to divide it into smaller groups of six to twelve persons each. One person in each smaller group should be appointed facilitator to keep the discussion alive. The facilitator can be either an adult or another young person. Advise the leaders not to try and dominate the group, but to be on the same level with each member. If the group looks to the facilitator for the answer, have the leader direct the questions or responses back to the group. Once the smaller groups have completed their discussions, have them reassemble into one large group, move through the items again, and ask the different sections to summarize what they learned from each activity.

It is not necessary to divide up into groups every time TalkSheets are used. Variations provide more interest. You may prefer, at times, to have smaller groups of the same sex.

The discussion should center around the questions and answers on the TalkSheet. Go through them one at a time, asking volunteers to share how they responded to each item. Have them compare their answers and brainstorm new ones in addition to those they wrote down. Allow those who don't feel comfortable revealing their answers to remain silent.

Don't feel pressured to spend time on each activity. If time does not permit a discussion of every item, feel free to focus attention only on those provoking the higher interest.

Move with your own creative instinct. If you discover a better or different way to use the activity, do so. Don't feel restricted by the Leader's Instructions on the back of the TalkSheet. Use Scriptures not found on the TalkSheet. Add your own items. TalkSheets were designed for you to be able to add your own thoughts and ideas.

If the group begins digressing into an area that has nothing to do with the topic, guide them back on track. However, if there is a high degree of interest in this side issue, you may wish to allow the extra discussion. It may meet a need of many in the group, and therefore would be worth pursuing.

More information on leading discussions is found in the next section.

Wrap up the discussion. This is your chance to challenge the group. When considering your closing remarks, ask yourself the following question: What do you want the group to remember from this experience? If you can answer in two or three sentences, then you have your closing remarks. It is important to bring some sort of closure to the session without negating the thoughts and opinions expressed by the group. A good wrap-up should affirm the group and offer a summary that helps tie the discussion together. Your students should be left with the desire to discuss the issue further, among themselves or with a leader. Tell your group members you are available to discuss the issue privately after the meeting. In some cases, a wrap-up may be unnecessary; just leave the issue hanging and bring it up again at a later date. This allows your students to wrestle with the issues on their own. Later, resolutions can evolve.

Follow up with an additional activity. The Leader's Instructions on the back of the TalkSheet provide you with ideas for additional activities. They are optional but highly recommended. Their purpose is to afford an opportunity to reflect upon, evaluate, review, and integrate what has been learned. Most of your TalkSheet discussions will generate a desire to discuss the subject matter again, which leads to better assimilation and more learning.

Assign the activity and follow up on the assignment with a short, debriefing talk at the next group meeting. Appropriate questions about the activity could be:

1. What happened when you did this activity? Was it helpful or a waste of time?
2. How did you feel while you were doing the activity?
3. Did the activity change your mind or affect you in any way?
4. In one sentence, tell what you learned from this activity.

HOW TO LEAD A TALKSHEET DISCUSSION

The young people of today are growing up in a world of moral confusion. The problem facing youth workers in the church is not so much how to teach the church's doctrines, but how to help kids make the right choices when faced with so many options. The church's response to this problem has traditionally been to indoctrinate—to preach and yell its point of view louder than the rest of the world. This kind of approach does not work in today's world. Teenagers are hearing a variety of voices and messages, most of which are louder than those they hear from the church.

A TalkSheet discussion is effective for just this very reason. While discussing the questions and activities on the TalkSheet, your students will be encouraged to think carefully about issues, to compare their beliefs and values with others, and will learn to make the right choices. TalkSheets will challenge your group to evaluate, defend, explain, and rework their ideas in an atmosphere of acceptance, support, and growth.

CHARACTERISTICS OF A TALKSHEET DISCUSSION

Remember, successful discussions—those that produce learning and growth—rarely happen by accident. They require careful preparation and sensitive leadership. Don't be concerned if you feel you lack experience at this time, or don't have the time to spend for a lengthy preparation. The more TalkSheet discussions you lead, the easier they will become and the more skilled you will be. It will help if you read the material on the next few pages and try to incorporate these ideas into your discussions.

The following suggestions will assist you in reaching a maximum level of success:

 Create a climate of acceptance. Most teenagers are afraid to express their opinions because they are fearful of what others might think. Peer approval is paramount with teenagers. They are fearful of being ridiculed or thought of as being dumb. They need to feel secure before they share their feelings and beliefs. They also need to know they can share what they are thinking, no matter how unpopular or wild their ideas might be. If any of your students are submitted to put-downs, criticism, laughter, or judgmental comments, especially if what they say is opposed to the teachings of the Bible or the church or their leader, an effective discussion will not be forthcoming.

For this reason, each TalkSheet begins with a question or activity less threatening and more fun than some of the questions that follow. The first question helps the individuals to become more comfortable with each other and with the idea of sharing their ideas more openly.

When asking a question, even one that is printed on the TalkSheet, phrase it to evoke *opinions*, not *answers*. In other words, if a question reads, "What should Bill have done in that situation?", change it to, "What *do you think* Bill should have done?" The addition of the three words "do you think" makes the question a matter of opinion rather than a matter of knowing the right answer. When young people realize their opinions are all that are necessary, they will be more apt to feel comfortable and confident.

 Affirm all legitimate expressions of opinion from your group members. Let each person know his or her comments and contributions are appreciated and important. This is especially true for those who rarely participate. When they do, make a point of thanking them. This will encourage them and make them feel appreciated.

Keep in mind affirmation does not necessarily mean approval. Affirm even those comments that seem like heresy to you. By doing so, you let the group know everyone has the right to express their ideas, no matter what they are. If someone does express an opinion that you believe is way off base and needs to be corrected, make a mental note of the comment and present an alternative point of view in your concluding remarks, in a positive way. Do not attack or condemn the person who made the comment.

 Discourage the group from thinking of you as the "authority" on the subject. Sometimes young people will think you have the right answer to every question and they will watch for your reaction, even when they are answering someone else's question. If you find the group's responses are slanted toward your approval, redirect them to the whole group. For example, you could say, "Talk to the group, not to me" or "Tell everyone, not just me."

It is important for you to try to let them see you as a *facilitator*—another member of the group who is helping make the discussion happen. You are not sitting in judgment of their responses, nor do you have the right answer to every problem.

Remember, with adolescents, your opinions will carry more weight the less of an authority figure you appear to be. If you are regarded as an affirming friend, they will pay much more attention to what you have to say.

4 Actively listen to each person. God gave you one mouth and two ears. Good discussion leaders know how to listen. Your job is not to monopolize the discussion, or to contribute the wisest words on each issue. Keep your mouth shut except when you are encouraging others to talk. You are a facilitator. You can express your opinions during your concluding remarks.

5 Do not force anyone to talk. Invite people to speak out, but don't attempt to force them to do so. Each member should have the right to pass.

6 Do not take sides during the discussion. Hopefully, you will have disagreements in your group from time to time with students who will take opposing viewpoints. Don't make the mistake of siding with one group or the other. Encourage both sides to think through their positions and to defend their points of view. You might ask probing questions of both, to encourage deeper introspection of all ideas. If everyone seems to agree on a question, or if they seem fearful of expressing a controversial point, it might be beneficial for you to play devil's advocate with some thought-provoking comments. This will force them to think. Do not give them the impression that the other point of view is necessarily your own, however. Remain neutral.

7 Do not allow one person (including yourself) to monopolize the discussion. Almost every group has that one person who likes to talk and is perfectly willing to express an opinion on every question. Try to encourage everyone to participate.

8 Arrange seating to encourage discussion. Theater-style seating, that is in rows, is not conducive to conversation. If you must use chairs at all, arrange them in a circular or semi-circular pattern.

Occasionally, smaller groups of four to six persons are less threatening to teenagers, especially if there is a variety of maturity levels in the group. If you have both junior high level and senior high level in the same group, it might be preferable to segregate them accordingly.

9 Allow for humor when appropriate. Do not take the discussion so seriously as to prohibit humor. Most TalkSheets include questions that will generate laughter as well as some intense dialogue.

10 Don't be afraid of silence. Many discussion leaders are intimidated by silence in the group. Their first reaction is to fill the silence with a question or a comment. The following suggestions may help you handle silence more effectively:

a. Learn to feel comfortable with silence. Wait it out for thirty seconds. Give someone a reasonable time to volunteer a response. If you feel it appropriate, invite a specific person to talk. Sometimes a gentle nudge is all that is necessary.

b. Discuss the silence with the group. Ask them what the silence really means. Perhaps they are confused or embarrassed and don't feel free to share their thoughts.

c. Answer the silence with questions or comments about it. Occasionally, comments such as "It's a difficult issue to consider, isn't it?" or "It's scary to be the first to talk" may break the ice.

d. Ask a different question that might be easier to handle or that might clarify the one that has been proposed. But don't do this too quickly. Wait a short while first.

11 Try to keep the discussion under control. Frequently a discussion can become sidetracked onto a subject you may not consider desirable. If someone brings up a side issue that generates a lot of interest, you will need to decide whether or not to pursue that issue and see where it leads, or redirect the conversation back to the original subject. Sometimes it's a good idea to digress—especially if the interest is high and the issue worth discussing. In most cases, however, it is advisable to say something like "Let's come back to that subject a little later, if we have time. Right now, let's finish our discussion on . . . "

12 Be creative and flexible. Don't feel compelled to ask every question on the TalkSheet, one by one, in order. If you wish, ask only a couple of them, or add a few of your own. The Leader's Instructions may give you some ideas, but think of your own as well. Each question may lead to several others along the same lines, which you can ask during the discussion.

13 Be an "askable" discussion leader. Make certain your young people understand they can talk to you about anything and find concern and support, even after the TalkSheet discussion has been completed.

14 Know what your goals are. A TalkSheet discussion should be more than just a bull session. TalkSheets are designed to move the conversation toward a goal, but you will need to identify that goal in advance. What would you like the young people to learn? What truth would you like them to discover? What is the goal of the session? If you don't know where you're going, it is doubtful you will arrive.

GROUND RULES FOR AN EFFECTIVE TALKSHEET DISCUSSION

A few ground rules will be helpful before beginning your TalkSheet discussions. Rules should be kept to a minimum, but most of the time young people will respond in a positive manner if they know in advance what is expected of them. The following are suggestions for you to consider using:

What is said in this room stays in this room. Confidentiality is vitally important to a healthy discussion. The only time it should be broken is if a group member reveals he or she is going to do harm to himself or herself, to another person, or is being harmed in some way.

No put-downs. Mutual respect is important. If someone disagrees with another's comment, he or she should raise his or her hand and express an opinion of the comment, but not of the person who made it. It is permissible to attack ideas, but not each other.

There is no such thing as a dumb question. Your youth and adult leaders must feel free to ask questions at any time. Asking questions is the best way to learn.

No one is forced to talk. Let everyone know they have the right to remain silent about any question.

Only one person talks at a time. This is one way to teach young people mutual respect. Each person's opinion is worthwhile and deserves to be heard.

   If members of the group violate these rules during the discussion or engage in disruptive or negative behavior, it would be wise to stop and deal with the problem before continuing.

THE BIBLE AND TALKSHEETS

Unlike previous TalkSheet books where Scripture was brought in to provide context to the topical discussion, this volume of TalkSheets is centered around key passages in Psalms and Proverbs. Utilizing vital topics as hooks, these TalkSheets are designed to provide you with a creative way to help your kids to dig more deeply into the Bible.

A WORD OF CAUTION . . .

Many of the TalkSheets in this book deal with topics which may be sensitive or controversial. Discussing subjects such as abortion or even materialism may not be appreciated by everyone in the church. Whenever you encourage discussion on such topics, or encourage young people to express their opinions (on any subject) no matter how off base they may be, you risk the possibility of criticism from parents or other concerned adults in your church. They may believe you are teaching the youth group heresy or questionable values.

The best way to avoid problems is to use good judgment. If you have reason to believe a particular TalkSheet is going to cause problems, think twice before you use it. Sometimes the damage done by going ahead outweighs the potential good.

Another way to avoid misunderstanding is to provide parents and others to whom you are accountable with copies of the TalkSheet before you use it. Let them know what you hope to accomplish and the type of discussion you will be encouraging.

It would also be wise to suggest your young people to take their TalkSheet home and discuss it with their parents. They might want to ask their parents how they would answer some of the questions.

WHICH WAY DO I GO ?

1 Read **Joshua 24:14, 15** and **Matthew 12:30**. What life-changing choices are presented in these passages?

2 Read **Psalm 1**. Complete the sentence below in your own words as though you were trying to explain the psalm to someone who did not understand it:

"Blessed [happy, to be envied] is the man who does not _____
or stand in the _____ or sit in the _____.
But his delight is in _____, and on God's law he _____."

3 Which of the following positive steps can be found in **Psalm 1:1-2**? Check the ones that seem to fit what the passage is saying:

a.____ Always seek and follow godly advice.
b.____ Surround yourself with godly, Christian friends.
c.____ Instead of ignoring God, fill your mind with him and thank him for everything he does.
d.____ The Bible has exciting, life-changing truths! Get to know it and obey it.
e.____ People who ridicule God don't really know what he is like. Get to know him!
f.____ To be really blessed, choose God's way.

4 The positive steps mentioned above are great to use in real life! Take a look at the following situations, where important choices must be made. Describe which of the steps above apply to each situation and what you would say to the person in need of help.

SUE never seems to have an opinion of her own. She always parrots what other people say. If she's with wise people, she thinks clearly; if she's in bad company, she stumbles. **Chad** likes to drink. He knows what everyone says: It's wrong and eventually it'll cause him problems. He wonders if they're right, but he's not sure and he doesn't know how to make up his mind.

RANDY was a passenger in a car crash in which a friend was killed and another disfigured. Randy believes in God but is angry at him. How could God allow something like this to happen? Randy may reject his faith in God.

TRINA dresses in a provocative way, so much so that even some of the guys think she's weird. She's thinking of buying several new outfits.

5 Rate yourself on how well you're doing in choosing to go God's way in life by placing an X on the graph below:

|_____|_____|_____|_____|_____|_____|_____|_____|
I'm going my way.   **I'm going God's way.**

13

WHICH WAY DO I GO?

Topic: Choosing to go God's way.
Biblical Basis: Psalm 1

Purpose of this Session:
The first psalm deals directly with life's most important issue: Choosing to live as God wants us to. Godly living is the ultimate target of all Christian teaching. With that transforming purpose in mind, this TalkSheet gives your students a look at what godliness is and some steps to obtain it.

To Introduce the Topic:
Ask your students to shout out some of the hard decisions in life that people their age are facing. They might suggest anything from what college to attend to whether or not to use drugs. Have volunteers share the smartest and dumbest decisions they've made in these areas. Explain that life is full of choices, some of which can be difficult to make. Move into the lesson by pointing out that God has placed the ultimate choice in everyone's path—to live for him or to ignore him.
 Explain that this discussion will reveal steps to take to successfully make the choice to go God's way.

The Discussion:
Item #1: The two passages center on choosing to go God's way rather than some false or useless way. Allow students to tell what the passages are about, then ask, "Is choosing to live for God an easy or hard thing to do?" Have students explain their answers.
Item #2: Be sure your class members understand these things: The psalm speaks against lending an open ear to tempting words or wicked advice, following others into sin, and mocking (ridiculing or ignoring) God. There is wisdom in basing one's life on God's wisdom found in the Bible.
Item #3: All of the steps involved in choosing God's way are at least alluded to in the passage. Explain that by "positive steps," you mean steps that people who want to walk with God can take to be blessed (leading happy, meaningful lives). To help explain the third and fifth steps, point out that thanking God will help them think of him often, prayer and trust will help them get to know him.
 Ask the students, "Is there any one step that is less important than the others or that can be safely ignored?"
Item #4: These situations give your students a chance to think ahead about meaningful ways to deal with similar situations they may encounter. Lead a discussion on these scenarios that centers around practical advice that your students could really use.
Item #5: Suggest that each person consider whether or not he or she needs to improve or wants to improve.

To Close the Session:
Summarize the steps in Item #3. They are: Seek and follow godly advice; keep godly friends; think of God (thanking him helps to do this); read and obey the Bible; get to know God (through prayer and trust); choose to go God's way as a habit. Make sure everyone understands that godliness results when people practice these things.

Outside Activity:
Give the students a moment of silence to examine how well they are doing in the six steps listed in Item #3. Have each person jot down on the back of the TalkSheet one area he or she has determined to improve this week. You can help get the wheels turning by sharing one area in your life that you will work on. For example, you might say, "The step that really speaks to me is the part about thanking God instead of ignoring him. I have so much to be thankful for, so every day this week I will wake up and thank God for something he has done for me."

When Things Go Wrong

1

TRUE or FALSE?

a. The Bible promises that Christians will never have troubles.   True ____ False ____

b. The Bible makes it clear that Christians can't find peace from problems until they go to heaven.   True ____ False ____

c. Any Christian struggling with growing up in the teen years is not a very good Christian.   True ____ False ____

d. Great Christians, like those in the Bible, never have worries because they can sit back and watch God solve everything.   True ____ False ____

e. Even the greatest believers must learn to trust God in times of trouble.   True ____ False ____

2

Read John 16:33. What does Jesus say about Christians and **problems**? What does Jesus say about **peace**?

3

Read Psalm 3. It tells us that God is a **shield**, that he **"bestows glory"** on us (helps us win against the odds), **takes care** of us, **answers prayer**, **sustains** us (keeps us going), **fights** on our behalf, **delivers** us, and **blesses** us. Follow the instructions in each situation below.

a. Gloria has worked hard to pass a very difficult math test. Which three factors above do you think would most encourage Gloria as she studies and worries?

b. Roberto is having a terrible time finding a summer job, which he and his family need. How could the fact that "God keeps us going" work in Roberto's favor?

c. Gina and Bill have vowed to abstain from sex until marriage, but the temptation is there. It doesn't help that their friends have teased them about it. In what way might the fact that "God blesses us" figure into Gina's and Bill's ability to wait? Choose two other factors and describe how they also could help.

4

Look up the following Scriptures and rate yourself accordingly:

	That's Me				That's Not Me
Matthew 6:25-26	1 •	2 •	3 •	4 •	5
John 14:27	1 •	2 •	3 •	4 •	5
Philippians 4:6-7	1 •	2 •	3 •	4 •	5
Colossians 3:15	1 •	2 •	3 •	4 •	5

5

Write a prayer either asking God to help you trust him more as you face problems, or thanking God for the trust and peace you do experience.

WHEN THINGS GO WRONG

Topic: Trusting God.
Biblical Basis: Psalm 3

Purpose of this Session:
The pressures high schoolers face today! Rapid change, stress, confusion, peer pressure, temptation—how can anyone come through it in one piece? God can get teenagers through it all, serving as their protector and deliverer just as he did to King David so long ago. During this session, students will learn that they can place their confidence in God, in whom they will find peace.

To Introduce the Topic:
Have your students think of as many sources of stress as they can. List them on the chalkboard. Illustrate the effects of stress using either of these suggestions:
   1. Place a walnut in a large C-clamp. As you read each source of stress listed, tighten the clamp a little. Do this until the nut is crushed.
   2. Have each item on the "stress list" represented by a student. A male volunteer comes to the front of the room. Every time you read an item from the list, the student representing that stress stands to the side of the volunteer and puts his or her arms tightly around him. Do this for eight or more of the stresses mentioned, until the volunteer is so tightly bound he can hardly move. (Just make sure he can breathe!)
   When finished with either demonstration, point out that life can be pressured during the high school years, but God can help.

The Discussion:
Item #1: Allow the students to debate the statements. Explain that these questions will be tackled during the session.
Item #2: Jesus said that all Christians will have problems on earth, but that there is peace for those who take refuge in him. Tell your students that peace does not mean a lack of problems, but the assurance that God will stand with us and help us work through them.
Item #3: Before moving to this step, you may wish to summarize the story of Absolom, David's son who rebelled against him and the reason he wrote Psalm 3. The story is found in 2 Samuel 15-18. Telling the story to your students will help them understand that God is someone we can turn to even in the darkest moments.
   Break your group into smaller discussion clusters for this item. If time permits, let each cluster work on all of the situations. Otherwise, assign one to each cluster.
Item #4: Allow the students to evaluate their "peace quotient." Remind students that peace is not an absence of problems, but a heartfelt knowledge that God is walking with us through our struggles.
Item #5: Give volunteers a chance to share their prayers.

To Close the Session:
Encourage your students to run to God when real trials come, rather than away from him. Troubles come, but God is always there to help us keep going.
   Make yourself available to those who want advice and prayer.

Outside Activities:
   1. Take the "stress list" created at the beginning of class and use it as the focus of a special prayer meeting that your students will attend this week.
   2. Have the students produce a skit for your junior high group entitled, "When Things Go Wrong." The three situations covered in Item #3 may provide some inspiration.

Valuable To God!

1 Can you answer this one: **What is it that gives a human life value?**

2 Read **Psalm 8.** What is the question David the author asks in verse 4? What does it mean?

3 David lists some of the terrific things God has done for us. Explain each in your own words, then find your favorite and circle it.

God made us just one step lower than angels. _____

God crowned us with glory and honor. _____

He set us up as rulers over everything else on earth. _____

He put us in charge of the earth's resources. _____

4 Read **John 3:16**. Because of his great love for us, what did God do?

_____

What **wonderful blessing** do we receive? _____

What do your two answers tell you about how valuable you are to God?

5 Take a look at **Romans 8:31-32**. What three things in these two verses show that God cares for us?

❶

❷

❸

Now look at verses 35-39. Will God's love for us and the high value he places on us ever go away?

6 Now quickly list all of the things God has done for us, mentioned in the above activities.

In **one** or **two** words, describe how this high value makes you feel: _____ .

VALUABLE TO GOD!

Topic: God values us.
Biblical Basis: Psalm 8

Purpose of this Session:
This TalkSheet gives your group a look at the high value that God places on each person. This value—which is found in God, not our own merits—makes life worthwhile and meaningful.

To Introduce the Topic:
Have your group call out several of the most popular songs on the radio. List them on the chalkboard. Working together with your students, figure out which songs either place value on a person (a love song, for instance) or seem to devalue people (songs that advocate violence or substance abuse). For the songs that value people, ask your students to determine why the singer values the other person—good reasons or faulty ones? Some love songs may really be about sexuality or outward appearance, rather than true human value.

Explain that today's session will discuss the real reasons why people have genuine value and why each person's life is purposeful and meaningful.

The Discussion:
Item #1: The way your students answer this question will reveal their philosophies and priorities. Some may have a hard time responding. If so, try this object lesson: Show your class a dollar bill and ask them to explain why it has value (or meaning and purpose). The dollar has no real value in and of itself—the paper and ink—but has value because people can use it to accomplish important things. This should help your students begin to grasp the fact that people are valuable because God attaches value to us and can use us to accomplish important things.
Item #2: After your students have read the psalm, summarize its various sections: The first part speaks of God's majesty; in the second David wonders how such a great God could care about mere humanity; the third section lists some of the wonderful things God has done for us.
Item #3: Allow your students to express their thinking. Talk about the students' reasons for circling the ones they did.
Item #4: By now, your class members should be convinced that God places a very high value on each of them. Help them to understand that because God values us, we are truly valuable and our lives are therefore meaningful.
Item #5: Use this passage to focus on the permanency of God's high valuation. Point out that God's love is based on his nature, not our merits. It doesn't matter how much money we have or don't have, our IQ, or how good or bad looking we may be. God loves us and is willing to accept us into his kingdom and family if we wish.

To Close the Session:
Now that you've led your students to a positive view of God's feelings towards them, ask this question: "Why should you value yourself and other people?" The answer is, "Because God does!"

Close by expressing your love for your students. Tell them that they are each of real value to the group and you appreciate the thought and feeling they put into the class discussions. Pray for the members of your class, thanking God for demonstrating how much he values us by doing the things you've studied today.

Outside Activities:
1. Have your students search the Gospels for examples of how Jesus showed people that he valued them. Almost any chapter will contain examples. Students should glean what Jesus did, reporting what they find at your next meeting.
2. With your students, take a "tour" through your church bulletin, finding ministries and programs that in some way honor people. A prayer meeting, for instance, honors people by praying for their needs. A small Bible study group honors people by helping them to learn more about God. A church potluck honors people by welcoming them into fun fellowship. Your students can see that in Christianity, people are valued and honored simply because they are God's people.

HOW TO BE A FULL-ON FOOL

1 Rate the following situations from the **most foolish** to ignore **(1)** to the **least foolish** to ignore **(10)**:

a.____ A traffic signal at a busy intersection
b.____ An ugly mole that suddenly appears on your skin
c.____ A woman who will sell you her husband's Corvette for $5 because she's mad at him
d.____ The Bible
e.____ Your dog when it begs to go outside
f.____ The school tardy bell
g.____ The oil warning light on your car
h.____ Those little black flags they put on the gnarliest ski slopes
i.____ Your mom's advice to wear a jacket
j.____ The voice that says, "Attention, shoppers. . . "

2 a. Read **Psalm 14**. What is it that the fool denies, according to verse 1?

b. Now read **Matthew 7:24-27**. What did the foolish man do in verses 26-27?

c. Why would that be the same as ignoring Jesus' words?

3 Is it possible to **believe in God** and **give your life to God** but still **ignore him?** Why or why not?

4 Based on what you've learned today, write a one-sentence description of how a person can be a **"FULL-ON FOOL"**:

5 Now that you have a good idea of what a fool is, take a look at this list from the Bible of things a fool does. Rate yourself, if you dare.

	That's Me	Now and Then	Never
Talks his way into trouble (Proverbs 10:8)	_____	_____	_____
Gossips (Proverbs 10:18)	_____	_____	_____
Takes pleasure in sin (Proverbs 10:23	_____	_____	_____
Ignores good advice (Proverbs 12:15)	_____	_____	_____
Gets angry fast; gets in fights (Proverbs 12:16)	_____	_____	_____
Lives a self-destructive life (Proverbs 14:1)	_____	_____	_____
Doesn't care who gets hurt (Proverbs 14:9)	_____	_____	_____
Is reckless (Proverbs 14:16)	_____	_____	_____
Ignores parental discipline (Proverbs 15:5)	_____	_____	_____
Wastes money (Proverbs 17:16)	_____	_____	_____
Likes to blab uninformed opinions (Proverbs 18:2)	_____	_____	_____
Doesn't save or plan for the future (Proverbs 21:20)	_____	_____	_____
Is lazy (Ecclesiastes 4:5)	_____	_____	_____

HOW TO BE A FULL-ON FOOL

Topic: The fool ignores God.
Biblical Basis: Psalm 14

Purpose of this Session:
What is a fool? According to Psalm 14:1, a person who says in his heart, "There is no God" is a fool. This TalkSheet will alert students to the dangers of ignoring God—a mistake even Christians can make.

To Introduce the Topic:
Tell the story of Sir William Osler, professor of medicine at Oxford University. Lecturing his young students on the importance of observing details, he showed them a bottle of urine and said, "This bottle contains a sample for analysis. It's often possible by tasting to determine the disease from which the patient suffers."

Dipping a finger into the urine, he brought his hand to his mouth and licked his finger. He then passed around the bottle. The students dutifully and gingerly sampled the urine. Doctor Osler retrieved the bottle and startled his students by saying, "Now you will understand what I mean when I speak about details. Had you been observant, you would have seen that I put my index finger in the bottle but my middle finger into my mouth!" (Story courtesy of *Hot Illustrations for Youth Talks*, Wayne Rice, 1994, Youth Specialties.)

These students ignored their professor at their own peril, and paid the price. Today's session deals with the foolish mistake of ignoring God.

The Discussion:
Item #1: Discuss the students' responses. Have students suggest possible consequences to ignoring the various situations, including God's Word. Point out that, while it is pretty foolish to ignore most of these situations, ignoring the Bible is by far the worst.
Item #2: In Psalm 14, God calls the one who denies him a fool. In Matthew 7:24-27, Jesus says that the person who ignores (hears but does not obey) his words is a fool. Discuss the imagery that Jesus used: the lack of surefootedness, the pressures, the failure. Make sure students understand that it is not just hearing Christ's words but obeying them that makes the difference.
Item #3: Unhappily, Christians can and do ignore God. Help your students to see that a habit of ignoring God is a sign of deep spiritual troubles.
Item #4: Let volunteers read their definitions of a fool.
Item #5: Have volunteers share how they fared on the assignment. Ask questions like: Are these problems common among teens? Would a person who behaved in these ways be considered a fool by most teens? What is the opposite of each foolish action? Do you know people who set positive examples in these areas?

To Close the Session:
Point out the progression of foolishness: (1) Deny or ignore God, (2) Disobey God, (3) Wind up doing foolish things. Explain that the only way to avoid being a fool in God's eyes is to open up to him, read the Bible, and practice doing what it says.

Outside Activities:
1. Encourage students to read their Bibles daily by working with them to develop a reasonable Bible reading assignment. There are many excellent daily devotionals available for high school students that can help you do this.
2. Have each person pick an area from the list of things a fool does that he or she has trouble with (laziness, arguments, gossip and so on). Let everyone choose a time frame (one week, two weeks, etc.) in which they will work on overcoming their problem. Call your teens to see how they are doing; you can encourage them and form a deeper relationship at the same time.

How To Be A Super Winner!

1 Figure out what you would like to be if your wildest dreams could come true! Look at the list of talents and traits and **check off the ones you would need in order to be a winner in your chosen field.**

_____Great singing voice
_____Super good looks
_____Big muscles
_____Good hand-eye coordination
_____Terrific education
_____Great "stage presence"
_____Lots of brains
_____Clear skin
_____Stamina
_____Outgoing personality

_____Good teeth
_____The right clothes
_____Musically talented
_____Poetic
_____Great memory
_____Sense of humor
_____Strong bones
_____Loud voice
_____Good knowledge of politics
_____Good reader

Any others?: _____

2 Write a C next to all the traits above that you think would make a Christian a super winner in God's sight.

3 **Psalm 15** lists traits that God looks for in people. List the traits mentioned in the following verses:

Verse 2:_____and_____and_____.
Verse 3:_____and_____and_____.
Verse 4:_____and_____and_____.
Verse 5:_____and_____.

To help define these traits in **modern** terms, circle the phrases below that paraphrases a trait mentioned above; cross out the ones that don't match.

A GODLY PERSON . . .

Doesn't gossip
Is a good person
Is generous
Is good looking
Enjoys the finer things
   in life

Doesn't cheat or lie
Doesn't eat too much
Stands by the innocent
Achieves high status
Partners with people who
   love God

Speaks well of other people
Influences others
Treats other people kindly
Keeps promises
Doesn't partner with people
   who love to sin

4 **True or false:**

a. It is possible to be a huge success as a rock star, super model, or sports hero without any of the godly traits listed in Psalm 15.

TRUE _____   FALSE _____

b. It is possible for a Christian to have none of the traits of Psalm 15 and still be a godly winner.

TRUE _____   FALSE _____

c. Not everyone can develop worldly talents, but everyone can enjoy godly traits if they go God's way.

TRUE _____   FALSE _____

5 Put a check mark by each godly trait you think you are doing well at. Print your initials by the godly traits you want to work on.

HOW TO BE A SUPER WINNER!

Topic: Godliness.
Biblical Basis: Psalm 15

Purpose of this Session:
Sports heroes, rock stars, power brokers—are these people winners? God has a different definition. A good example of what he calls a winner is given in Psalm 15. This TalkSheet provides you with an opportunity to set some young lives on the path to real success. Students will discover eleven attributes of godliness, God's definition of a winner.

To Introduce the Topic:
Have six volunteers come forward. Each pair is to act out a 30-second skit that you narrate.

In the first one, have two boys do a slow motion boxing match. Call out each punch that the boys throw in turn, always calling for the same boy to land damaging blows while the other boy always misses. It might go something like this: "John lands a powerful punch to Pete's belly. Pete doubles over in pain. Courageously, Pete swings but misses by three feet. John hits him three times on the nose. Pete goes down. Our new world champion, John!" John returns to his seat like a champ, Pete is to act miserable and injured.

Next, two girls play dancers competing for a role in a Broadway play. According to your narration, they both do a great job auditioning. You then play the director who praises one and horrendously ridicules the other. One girl is to act proud, the other depressed and miserable as they return to their seats.

The final skit is a spelling bee. Ask the winner to spell "cat" and the loser to spell "Qizilchoqa," a place in China meaning "Red Hillock." Even if the loser happens to understand Chinese and gets it right, scream, "Wrong!" and have everyone boo the loser as he or she sits down.

Ask students what these three skits have in common. They have winners and losers. Say something like, "The topic of winning and losing is very interesting to us. I want to be a winner and I want you to be winners. The three skits showed winners and losers as some people might define the terms. But God has a completely different definition! Let's discuss what winning really is in God's eyes and see if we can learn how to be genuine winners."

The Discussion:
Item #1: Discuss what the students have done. Have your class name a few "super winners" that have some of the traits listed. It is likely that no one will mention a Bible character. If not, point this out and ask students if they think that there are no winners in the Bible. Have them work on the next step.
Item #2: Explain that God has a list of traits that he admires in a person, but they are considerably different than those listed in Item #1. None of the traits there match the godly traits of Psalm 15.
Item #3: This exercise will help your teens realize that the world's definition of a winner is considerably different from the things God values in a person. Note: Students will probably wonder about verse 4, which speaks of despising a vile man. We know from the rest of the Bible that this is not hatred we harbor for another, but a strong refusal to partnership in the sins of others.
Item #4: The last true/false is the one to focus on here. Encourage your students to recognize that the ability to be a winner in God's eyes is open to everyone willing to go God's way, no matter who they are.
Item #5: Give volunteers an opportunity to tell which traits they would like to develop.

To Close the Session:
Challenge the students to think of what kind of world we would live in if everyone practiced godly traits. Tell them that there are enough students in their class to make a real difference at school—just a handful of kids actively living to please God can have a real impact on campus.

Outside Activities:
Turn everyone into GTDs—Godly Trait Detectives. They are to look for instances of godly traits being displayed or broken during the coming week. For example, they may notice someone gossiping, or refusing to pass on a bit of gossip. Volunteers can report at the next meeting (changing the names to protect the innocent).

count your blessings

1 What do you think the word *"blessed"* means? Give a one- or two-word answer.

_____

2 On the list below, place an **X** beside the things you consider yourself blessed with:

_____ Good friends	_____ Athletic ability
_____ High IQ	_____ A safe neighborhood
_____ A bright future	_____ Sunny personality
_____ A good family	_____ Talent (musical, artistic, etc.)
_____ Money	_____ Even temperament
_____ Health	_____ Other: _____

3 I am blessed (choose one):

_____ **More than most people I know**

_____ **About the same as most people I know**

_____ **Less than most people I know**

4 Read **Psalm 16**. Starting with verse 5, find seven blessings and rewrite them in your own words:

Verse 5: _____

Verse 5: _____

Verse 6: _____

Verse 10: _____

Verse 11: _____

Verse 11: _____

Verse 11: _____

5 Here are more blessings God gives to Christians, all mentioned in a letter the apostle Paul wrote to the church at Ephesus. Circle the responses that show where you stand at this time in your life:

★ God picked us out individually to enjoy him before the world was even created	**That's me!**	**Not sure**	**Nope**
★ He adopted us as children into his forever family	**That's me!**	**Not sure**	**Nope**
★ He redeemed (purchased) us and forgave all our sins	**That's me!**	**Not sure**	**Nope**
★ He saved us	**That's me!**	**Not sure**	**Nope**
★ He gave us the Holy Spirit to live in our hearts	**That's me!**	**Not sure**	**Nope**
★ We have an inheritance (a place and a reward) in heaven	**That's me!**	**Not sure**	**Nope**
★ We have access (through prayer) to Almighty God	**That's me!**	**Not sure**	**Nope**

COUNT YOUR BLESSINGS

Topic: Blessings.
Biblical Basis: Psalm 16

Purpose of this Session:
Young people need to hear and see adults like you expressing the joys, pleasures, and benefits of walking with God. David gave us a wonderful list of blessings when he wrote Psalm 16. As you go through it with your students you can tell them why you can say, "My heart is glad and my tongue rejoices" (Psalm 16:9).

   We know there are times when it is hard to feel happy or blessed. Those times are not in sight in this psalm nor in this TalkSheet; they can be discussed in other sessions.

To Introduce the Topic:
Choose two students to roleplay a "pity party." They are bored, depressed, and complaining. They complain about school, chores, parents, blind dates, anything they want. At the end they say something like, "Life is miserable!" Addressing the class, you chime in with, "Have you ever felt like this? Well, don't worry! Be happy! Because. . . " Explain that today's discussion centers on the wonderful blessings that Christians are privileged to enjoy.

The Discussion:
Item #1: Ask volunteers to give their definitions. Explain that in the Bible the word "blessed" most often means happy or to be envied. A person who is blessed, then, is a person in a happy, enviable position because God has done wonderful things for him or her.
Item #2: Point out that these are things people around the world would consider good blessings.
Item #3: Although the blessings of Item #2 are good to have, we recognize that not everyone receives all of them; some people might have only a few or possibly none of them. But as your students will see in the next step, God does provide guaranteed blessings every believer can enjoy. (If you have any students who feel they have been left behind in the blessings department, encourage them that God has not forgotten them, as they will see.)
Item #4: Discuss each blessing and help students relate the principles to their lives. Knowing what direction to go in life (verse 11), for instance, gives a person a huge advantage over someone who is aimless and drifting. Psalm 16 is just a tiny sample of the many Bible passages that speak of the wonderful gifts Christians can enjoy. Some class members may be able to think of other blessings the Bible mentions.
Item #5: Without calling on students to reveal specific answers, discuss each blessing in turn, being sure everyone understands the meaning and significance of each. Help class members realize that the blessings of Psalm 16 are for all believers. Explain to them that it is possible to miss out on these blessings if we have not put ourselves in a position to be blessed. That positon is at God's side, following him.

To Close the Session:
Lead the class in prayer, thanking God for each blessing that has been discussed. Encourage the students to form a habit of "counting their blessings" and thanking God daily for the goodness he shows them.

Outside Activities:
   1. Give a "Write Your Own Psalm" assignment. Students are to come up with their own praise psalm, similar to Psalm 16.
   2. Collect a stack of magazines from which your students can clip photos, headlines, and drawings that illustrate ordinary and extraordinary blessings that God provides. Make a giant collage.

victory!

1 List the two or three most difficult challenges high school kids face:

2 Read **Psalm 20**. Match the phrases on the left with the idea they convey on the right.

PSALM 20 SAYS . . .	AND IT'S KIND OF LIKE . . .
May the Lord answer you in your distress.	God's soldiers fight along with you.
May the name of God protect you.	God makes sure you reach your battle objectives.
May God send you help and support.	Some people try to fight with crummy pea shooters.
May God remember all your sacrifices.	His name is like an indestructible shield.
May God accept your burnt offerings.	Your battle plans are better than the enemy's.
May God give you the desire of your heart.	Our Commander-in-Chief can crush any enemy.
May God make your plans succeed.	The Lord is there to help you when you dial 911.
We will shout and wave banners when you win.	God remembers you've trusted your life to him.
Some trust in chariots and horses.	God accepts your desire to surrender to him.
We trust in God.	We're going to celebrate your victory!

3 Psalm 20 offers encouragement to people facing the challenges you listed at the beginning. Sum up that encouragement in one sentence:

_____

4 Pick one of the situations below and answer these questions:

- *What are the most important steps the person or persons must take to achieve the goal?*
- *What are things the person or persons must not do to achieve the goal?*
- *How can God help out at each step?*

a. Kerry likes to date. Her desire is to keep her dating life wholesome and fun.

b. Skye wants to lead her best friend to Christ.

c. Linda has decided to stay away from alcohol. But some of her friends drink, especially at parties.

d. Juan, Larry, and Judi are best friends. School morale is at an all-time low due to violence, drugs, etc. The three friends want to work to improve things.

5 What is one important challenge or goal in your life? How could God help you walk through your challenge or meet your goal?

VICTORY!

Topic: Facing challenge.
Biblical Basis: Psalm 20

Purpose of this Session:
Young people face significant challenges in their daily lives. Some challenges arise in the area of temptation: drugs, sex, depression. Other challenges are more positive: striving to do well in school, replacing a bad habit with a good one, leading a friend to Christ. In Psalm 20, David prayed for victory in battle. His prayer can show young people that the best way to face any challenge is at God's side.

To Introduce the Topic:
1. Tell your class about a difficult challenge you faced. Explain how God helped you through it or, if you weren't a Christian at the time, how you think God could have played a greater part in your struggle.
2. Present a challenge to your students: weight guessing contests, staring duel, arm wrestling, or the like. Tell your class that whenever a person is faced with a challenge, the result is either victory or defeat. God helps us to win.
3. Invite a person who faced a great challenge to describe the experience to your students.

The Discussion:
Item #1: Make a list of the top few challenges common to many of your students.
Item #2: Discuss every phrase, allowing students to suggest ways each thought relates to the subject of victory. (Sacrifices and burnt offerings speak of coming to God to be made right with him—trusting one's life to him—and the desire to surrender to him). Note the important ideas of prayer, clinging to God, trust, being right with God, and the need to have godly goals.
Item #3: Pick the best sentences and use them for Item #4.
Item #4: You can use the suggested situations, or simply talk about the top one or two challenges the students suggested in Item #1. Students should understand that goals can be real challenges. Lofty goals are not easily obtained. But God can help in real ways. God might help Kerry meet a godly guy who will treat her with respect. God could cause Linda to realize she might need to stay away from both the influence of her friends that drink and the parties that tempt her. Point out that there are many ways God can help a person face a tough challenge.
Item #5: This activity should be kept private, but volunteers may wish to share.

To Close the Session:
After encouraging everyone to strive with God to face the challenge or reach the goal they set in Item #5, have students share some victories they've experienced. Be ready to salt the conversation with a few examples of your own. Lead a prayer of thanksgiving to God.

Outside Activities:
1. If someone in your group has an exceptional challenge or goal, such as overcoming a severe injury or medaling in a sport, organize your class into a support group. Let your students determine when and for what they will pray, how they can encourage people in tangible ways, what events to attend, and so forth. Be sure your class members realize that God can and will work through their actions.
2. The Bible is full of stories of victory. If you have students who are learning to lead Bible studies, have one or more of them do so on this subject.

Follow the Leader

 1 Who would you say is the chief guide through life for most high school kids? (Circle your answer.)

God　　　**Self**　　　**Parents**　　　**Friends**　　　**Blind chance**　　　**Most have no guide**

 2 Read **Psalm 23**. Take a look at the problems below. Next to each, write out one verse from the psalm that speaks to the problem:

John has no idea what he wants to do when he graduates. He's very worried about his future.

Carly is only 16 and already she's stressed out; tons of schoolwork plus two jobs. She would feel very insecure if she eased up.

Estaban was raised in a strong church, but now his family doesn't go. He has a million questions about God and no answers.

Jenny is battling cancer; the prospects are 50/50.

 **3** Read **John 10:11-16**.

Who is the shepherd in this passage? _____

In what verse do you see yourself? _____

What are the sheep supposed to do? _____

What does it mean to listen? _____

 **4** Try this: Replace all references to the Lord in Psalm 23 with the other things listed in #1 above. How effective do you think these other guides would be compared to the Lord? Why?

 5 What kind of follower are you? Give yourself 100 points for each "That's me" answer; take away 100 points for each "That's not me."

	That's me	That's not me
a. I look to God for guidance.	___	___
b. I rarely worry.	___	___
c. I strive to live the Christian life.	___	___
d. I really like attending youth group.	___	___
e. I seek the advice of godly adults.	___	___
f. I like to pray.	___	___

 **6** Paraphrase your favorite one or two verses from Psalm 23, writing them as though the author was a good friend of yours telling you how to better follow the Good Shepherd:

_____

_____

FOLLOW THE LEADER

Topic: Following Christ.
Biblical Basis: Psalm 23

Purpose of this Session:

"The Lord is my shepherd"—some of the most famous words in the English language. Often read at graveside, it is a song for the living. Your students need the same guide that David enjoyed: the Lord. Psalm 23 paints the picture of care and guidance that the Lord provides and the world so desperately needs.

To Introduce the Topic:

Ask your students to name several great leaders who are alive today. They can choose political leaders, military leaders, influential business leaders, celebrities, even well-known sports leaders. Keep pressing until the class begins to run out of steam or some smart person says, "Jesus!" Point out that Jesus is very much alive today and is the leader of many people around the world and in your classroom.

The Discussion:

Item #1: Ask your students to honestly evaluate who leads them through life. Discuss the need for a guide in life. Talk about who the best guide is.

Item #2: Discuss each verse the students have chosen. As a group, define the meaning of key words and phrases in the psalm, such as shepherd, green pastures, and valley of death.

Item #3: Discuss the answers to the questions. Point out that to listen to Christ means to hear and obey—obedience is the key to following our Shepherd.

Item #4: It's nice to have parents and friends around when we are in trouble, but ultimately it is the Lord who is the only completely dependable source of comfort and guidance.

Item #5: This short test gives your students a chance to evaluate their spiritual temperature. Some students may volunteer their scores; otherwise, you can discuss the test questions in general terms. Ask questions like, "How does one look to God for guidance? What does it mean to live the Christian life? How often should a Christian pray?" If some kids feel they fall short, help them to see that even small steps of improvement over time is better than no improvement at all.

Item #6: Let volunteers read their paraphrases.

To Close the Session:

Encourage students to privately pick one area from Item #5 that they would like to do better at. Have each person choose one or two verses from Psalm 23 that apply to that area.

As a benediction, read Hebrews 13:20-21: "May the God of peace, who through the blood of the eternal covenant brought back from the dead our Lord Jesus, that great Shepherd of the sheep, equip you with everything good for doing his will, and may he work in us what is pleasing to him, through Jesus Christ, to whom be glory for ever and ever. Amen."

Outside Activities:

1. Have your students memorize this psalm. Let them know it will be useful all through their lives.

2. Have a "Guidance Night" at which students can present questions to you or a panel of godly adults. The questions should focus on knowing God's will, how high school students can serve God, and specific advice to students with particular talents or needs.

When Your Parents Let You Down

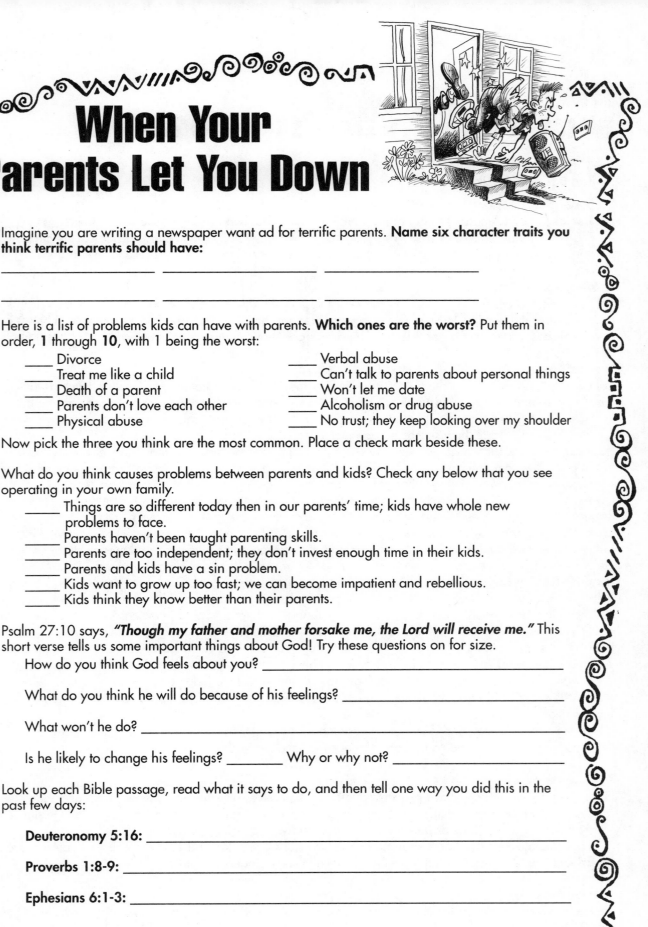

1 Imagine you are writing a newspaper want ad for terrific parents. **Name six character traits you think terrific parents should have:**

_____   _____   _____

_____   _____   _____

2 Here is a list of problems kids can have with parents. **Which ones are the worst?** Put them in order, **1** through **10**, with 1 being the worst:

____ Divorce
____ Treat me like a child
____ Death of a parent
____ Parents don't love each other
____ Physical abuse

____ Verbal abuse
____ Can't talk to parents about personal things
____ Won't let me date
____ Alcoholism or drug abuse
____ No trust; they keep looking over my shoulder

Now pick the three you think are the most common. Place a check mark beside these.

3 What do you think causes problems between parents and kids? Check any below that you see operating in your own family.

_____ Things are so different today then in our parents' time; kids have whole new problems to face.
_____ Parents haven't been taught parenting skills.
_____ Parents are too independent; they don't invest enough time in their kids.
_____ Parents and kids have a sin problem.
_____ Kids want to grow up too fast; we can become impatient and rebellious.
_____ Kids think they know better than their parents.

4 Psalm 27:10 says, *"Though my father and mother forsake me, the Lord will receive me."* This short verse tells us some important things about God! Try these questions on for size.

How do you think God feels about you? _____

What do you think he will do because of his feelings? _____

What won't he do? _____

Is he likely to change his feelings? _____ Why or why not? _____

5 Look up each Bible passage, read what it says to do, and then tell one way you did this in the past few days:

Deuteronomy 5:16: _____

Proverbs 1:8-9: _____

Ephesians 6:1-3: _____

WHEN YOUR PARENTS LET YOU DOWN

Topic: Problems with parents.
Biblical Basis: Psalm 27

Purpose of this Session:
For the first time in America, single-parent families outnumber two-parent families. Even teens with two parents can be part of families in crisis. This TalkSheet shows how God can fill the void and soothe the pain. In the church, God has provided adult men and women teens can look up to and receive love from.

To Introduce the Topic:
Tell the students about your parents. What were the good things they did? What were the bad? What is your relationship with them like today? Tell your group that parents are gifts from God, but they aren't perfect. Today's discussion focuses on problems with parents and ways to make things better.

The Discussion:
Item #1: As students discuss their want ads, be sure they are focusing on character traits (such as loving and loyal) rather than things like big bank accounts and willingness to pay a kid's long-distance phone bills.
    [Note: If someone mentions that his or her parents are really good ones, have the student share some of the things that make them successful parents.]
Item #2: Is there a difference between the worst problems and the most common? Talk about the things that might cause the common problems. Examples: Parents might wish to delay dating because they are afraid of consequences of unwise dating; a lack of trust may be deserved because of past disobedience.
Item #3: The root cause of family problems is the sinful nature that we all have. Our sinfulness can show itself through all of the problems listed and many more. Sometimes this sin is an active disregard for the ways of God, such as a father who does not care for the welfare of his family. Other times it can be a well-intended but wrong idea about how things should be done. It can even be problems caused by outside forces over which no family has control. These are all direct or indirect results of the fall of humankind.
Item #4: This verse promises that God is faithful even if parents are not. God loves your students. He can help troubled families. Sometimes he will change parents or children who need to improve, sometimes he provides comfort even though parents won't or can't change or improve. He can even bring loving Christian adults (such as you) into a teen's life to help heal pain and serve as a mentor and role model.
Item #5: As you assign this discussion item, tell your students, "We've talked about some of the problems parents and kids have, and some of the causes of these problems. We've seen that God cares and can intervene. Now let's look at three suggestions God has put in the Bible to help you prevent problems before they start. Following God's instructions won't mean you'll see all your problems solved, but you will cause far fewer in your family."
    Have your class read and discuss these passages one at a time. Have students suggest realistic ways parents could and should be honored, obeyed, and learned from.

To Close the Session:
Have everyone write one or two prayer requests for themselves and their parents on a slip of paper. These requests should focus on specific problems. The prayers can be anonymous or not. Collect all the slips and pray for them one at a time or redistribute them for individuals to pray aloud.
    Congratulate everyone for their input on this stressful subject. Remind your students that you are available for private talk. (You may wish to take the initiative in some students' cases.)

Outside Activity:
Have your students brainstorm a list of things the church can do to help families. This list can include parenting seminars, personal counseling, family Bible studies that address the issue of family problems, mother/daughter and father/son activities, special support groups, a Big Brother/Big Sister type of program and so forth. Then, have your group select one idea to put into effect. Present the proposal to your minister.

I LOVE YOU LORD

1 Rate how you feel about these thoughts. (Draw a line to appropriate responses. You can use feelings more than once or not at all.)

THOUGHTS:

Being a Christian
Talking to God
Talking about God
Attending these Bible discussions
Going to heaven
Serving God with my life
Learning more about God
Growing as a Christian
Loving God

FEELINGS:

Glad!   Love it!
Bored!   Hate it!
Excited!   Very enjoyable!
Confused!   Fun!
I can't wait!   Bail out!
Do I have to?   Don't care
What's the point?   Pahleeze. . .
Stoked!   Happy!
Why bother?   EEEEK!

2 Read **Psalm 37:4.**

What does it say to do? _____

What does it say will happen? _____

Do you think there are exceptions to this promise? _____

3 Write a sentence explaining what you think it means to **delight in the Lord:**_____

_____

4 Rewrite **Psalm 37:4**, replacing the word delight with at least five phrases describing ways to delight in God (see #1 above for some ideas):

5 List three things that you think would help a person delight in God. List three things that might prevent it. For example, a really good music concert that praises God would probably get people excited about God. What would dull music do?

DELIGHT   **PREVENT**

_____   _____

_____   _____

_____   _____

I LOVE YOU, LORD!

Topic: Delighting in God.
Biblical Basis: Psalm 37

Purpose of this Session:
Jesus said, "If you love me, you will obey what I command," (John 14:15). We teach our students to love God by faithful acts of obedience and service. But what about the emotional aspect of love for God? Psalm 37:4 is perhaps the best short description of a heartfelt love for God: "Delight yourself in the Lord . . . ". This TalkSheet gives your students the opportunity to discover the joys of delighting in God.

To Introduce the Topic:
Talk about (or hand out) something your teens would really enjoy, such as jelly donuts. Have them describe their emotional response in single words: happy, overjoyed, drooling, and so on. Tell students you are looking for one particular word that the Bible often uses to describe these sort of emotions. The word you are looking for, of course, is delight. If no one guesses, add some hints: "It starts with the letter D." Move into the class discussion by explaining that today's topic is delighting in, or enjoying, Almighty God.

The Discussion:
Item #1: This activity calls your students to evaluate their "delight factor." Ask students if they think most people their age are delighted by God.
Item #2: Have willing students share their answers. Make sure everyone knows that the promise of receiving the desires of our hearts does not mean we can have anything we want anytime we want. The verse means that not only will God give us the object of our desires, he will place his godly desires in our hearts first. These desires will not conflict with his will or nature.
Item #3: Get a good consensus of opinion and sum it up on the chalkboard.
Item #4: Ask students to read their paraphrases. Jot some of the better insights on the chalkboard.
Item #5: Have everyone describe what they've come up with. Positive suggestions may include answered prayers, meaningful worship, fun Bible studies, and quiet meditation. Encourage students to practice the positive suggestions and avoid the negative.

Are the students' positive suggestions practical? If so, perhaps your class will want to put some of them into practice as a group. See the Outside Activities section for an example.

To Close the Session:
1. On a poster or chalkboard, let your students list phrases that describe some of the terrific things that God has done for us, things that make us delight in God.
2. This alternative goes well with the second suggestion below. Give everyone a chance to record a "message to God" on a cassette recorder or video tape. Each student gets to say or shout one sentence: "I love you God, because . . . ."

Outside Activities:
1. Have kids search the Bible for examples of things God has done to delight us. Or, have them find as many names and titles of God as they can; these usually speak to God's delightful greatness.
2. Plan a "Jesus Celebration Party." Include music that joyfully celebrates great things God has done for us (Christian music videos are nice), several one-minute Bible talks that point out the greatness of God, a time to listen to the tape you made above, praise posters, Bible games, party favors, and so on.

RICH MAN, POOR MAN

1 Below is a list of "neat stuff" most people would like to own. On the line that follows each neat thing, write one phrase (from the list on the right) that tells why you may think the thing is valuable. Cross out the phrases as you use them, because you can only use them once.

NEAT STUFF

Big house _____

Nice car _____

Good teeth _____

Yacht _____

Airplane _____

Island hideaway _____

Private ski slope _____

Personal chef _____

Pile of money _____

Giant projection TV _____

Fabulous music collection _____

WHY IT'S NEAT

The better to smile with

The better to float with

Lots of room to live

Good place to exercise

Private beaches

Nice way to get to my island

Lasts for eternity

Security

Would make me popular

Great entertainment

I like to eat

2 Read at least one of the following passages from **Psalm 49**. In one sentence, tell the main thought of that passage:

Psalm 49:1-9 _____

Psalm 49:10-12 _____

Psalm 49:13-15 _____

Psalm 49:16-20 _____

3 After reading Matthew 6:19-21, think about the statements below. Check the ones you agree with.

_____ **There's a lot a kid my age can do to earn treasure in heaven.**

_____ **It's hard for a teenager to earn treasure in heaven.**

_____ **I could earn a lot of treasure, but it's really hard to go against all my friends who don't care.**

_____ **Who really cares about treasure in heaven? As long as I make it there, that will be good enough.**

4 Would you like to earn *real treasure* in heaven, stuff that you can enjoy forever? Here are some **ideas that God rewards**; circle two or three that you would be willing to try and would most enjoy.

Invite a new person to a fun youth group event

Memorize Scripture

Serve the youth group in some capacity

Join a youth group planning committee

Visit a sick person

Pray regularly for the youth leaders

Obey God's Word

Tell others what God has done for you

Raise funds for the group

Help pass out food to the hungry

Now we want to hear **YOUR** idea: _____

RICH MAN, POOR MAN

Topic: Eternal wealth.
Biblical Basis: Psalm 49

Purpose of this Session:
This TalkSheet is designed to teach young people practical ways to earn treasure in heaven. They'll have to earn the earthly stuff without our help.

To Introduce the Topic:
Show pictures of or describe expensive material possessions such as limousines, yachts, mansions, and planes. Say something like this: "These things would be fun to own, wouldn't they? Unhappily, I can't tell you how to earn these. But I can tell you how to earn even greater riches in heaven, because the Bible tells us how. The riches you earn in heaven will never go away; you'll be able to enjoy them forever."

An alternative is to ask your students to dream up some fanciful illustration of just how long eternity is (something like, "How long would it take a bird flying to and from the moon to transfer it one grain at a time to the surface of earth—that's one day in eternity"). The Bible tells how to be prepared for eternity.

The Discussion:
Item #1: Students will complain that they need another phrase to complete the assignment, because "Lasts for eternity" applies to none of the material possessions. Talk about the one drawback to the neat things: none of them lasts forever.
Item #2: Be sure each passage is assigned. The main thoughts you want your students to uncover are: Earthly wealth can't buy eternal life (vv. 1-9); wealth and life on earth are temporary (10-12); all die, there is hope only in God's redemption (13-15); nothing can be taken into eternity (16-20).

The sum total of the psalm is that material possessions are no substitute for the eternal life that God offers. In short, having things on earth is nice but having life in heaven is everything.
Item #3: Discuss each issue, encouraging kids to realize that God has no age requirements for earning treasure in heaven.
Item #4: Have volunteers share their ideas. Encourage everyone to follow through in the near future. The Outside Activities section offers a framework in which your students can do the things they've suggested.

To Close the Session:
Remind your group of the points discovered during the discussion. Stress the fact that wise people don't ignore the future, they strive for it and plan for it. Promote the idea that treasure can be earned on a daily basis by living the Christian life daily.

Outside Activities:
   1. Brainstorm a practical class project to involve everyone in some sort of heavenly reward-earning work. It can be simple or involved, whatever your teens are willing to commit to. Set a time and date and create job descriptions for all. Have a "debriefing" meeting afterward so students can be reminded of the reward they will receive.
   2. Have students keep a journal of things they do that they think are reward earning. Review them in a week or two and offer constructive criticism.

IS GODLINESS A WASTE OF TIME?

1 What things do you think **attract** people your age to Christianity?

_____

_____

_____

_____

2 Finish this sentence: "If I were to bail out on God, it would be because _____

_____

3 Read **Psalm 73**. Asaph, the author, nearly spun away from God. What are the three reasons he gives in verses 3, 12, and 14?

4 Was Asaph right? Is the life of an average non-Christian better than a Christian's? Rate the following areas by checking which answer applies to each:

	Christians	Non-Christians	Both or Neither
Happier people	_____	_____	_____
Better parties	_____	_____	_____
Higher quality fun	_____	_____	_____
More freedom	_____	_____	_____
Better friendships	_____	_____	_____
More satisfied	_____	_____	_____
Better future	_____	_____	_____
Fewer problems	_____	_____	_____

5 Why did Asaph decide to stay put with God? Check one or more of the following:

____ The greener grass had weeds.
____ He was afraid God would crunch him.
____ He knew that nonbelievers have no real future.
____ He knew God would come through.
____ The world, however attractive, meant less to him than God did.

6 Read verse 17 again. What was it that helped him turn back to God? Reword the verse to explain to a child what was really going on when Asaph entered the sanctuary.

_____

_____

_____

IS GODLINESS A WASTE OF TIME?

Topic: Staying on track with God.

Biblical Basis: Psalm 73

The Purpose of this Session:
The world can sometimes seem more fun than the Christian life. The attractions of the world will open a back-door to your youth group, even while new kids are coming in the front. Psalm 73 was written by a man who experienced a near-fatal crisis of faith as he observed the world around him. Asaph was able to stay on track, however. His words will give your students ammunition in their struggle to stick with God.

To Introduce the Topic:
Ask students to describe the best times they've ever had. Most will probably speak of special trips or amusement parks or the like; some may mention special youth group activities. Few if any will cite Bible studies or church services.

Point out that, while the Christian experience certainly has its fun and exciting moments, it also has quiet, serious times. Anyone who is in Christianity just for the thrills may not last. Today's discussion is based on the experiences of a man who almost fell away from God because he was momentarily attracted to the so-called greener pastures on the other side of the fence.

The Discussion:
Item #1: Let the group share its findings. List them on the board. Ask students to rate the "holding power" of each attraction. Are these things likely to keep someone interested for a lifetime, or is the person more likely to be going through a phase?

Item #2: Encourage students to think deeply about the things that might cause them to lose interest in their commitment to God. Some things that could spoil a Christian's commitment might come from inside the community ("too many hypocrites") and some from the outside ("a non-Christian girlfriend"). Encourage your students to understand that, while Christianity attracts a lot of people, people do wander away from it. Therefore, it pays to strengthen one's commitment and shield one's heart from outside distractions.

Item #3: Ask your group if the three reasons are still much the same today. Point out that verse 14's reference to punishment did not mean that God was being cruel, but that Asaph was suffering some long-term problem such as illness, poverty or depression.

Item #4: The purpose of this activity is not so much to choose a "winner" in the who's the happiest contest, but to show that Asaph's complaint over the seeming success of nonbelievers was valid. In some ways, the grass really does look greener "over there," until we see with spiritual eyes. A non-Christian's life can be a good one. But as the next step shows, their enjoyment will be terminated eventually.

Item #5: The only untrue statement is "He was afraid God would crunch him." It was Asaph's insight into the true nature of the nonbeliever's plight, his knowledge that God would eventually glorify him, and his love for God that kept him on the straight road. Go over these reasons carefully with your group, helping everyone to privately evaluate their own strength in these areas.

Item #6: Let volunteers share. It wasn't the sanctuary (temple) that did the trick; it was meeting God in the sanctuary. For modern believers, God's sanctuary is within us. When we meet God in our hearts where he can speak and work changes in us, we learn to toss away the world to live forever with God.

To Close the Session:
If you are familiar with your youth group's history, give an approximate ratio of the kids who have come in the "front door" and those who have fallen out the "back door". Review Asaph's reasons for sticking with God in the face of distractions. Emphasize that these are key tips that will help each person stay on track.

Outside Activity:
Have kids interview non-Christian friends with the question, "Why aren't you a Christian?" At your next meeting, have your students write the answers they received on the chalkboard or poster paper. Work with your group to come up with responses to these reasons. For example, if one answer was, "Because I can't have fun if I'm a Christian," figure out ways Christians can have fun and plan times to do these things together.

DOWN AND OUT

1 Read **Psalm 82:3-4**. Use a dictionary or your own knowledge to define these words from the passage:

Defend _____

Maintain _____

Rescue _____

Deliver _____

2 Give examples of the type of person (no names) who would qualify for these labels, also from Psalm 82:

Weak _____

Fatherless _____

Poor _____

Oppressed _____

Needy _____

3 How do you think most people your age would react if they saw someone who is lonely, defenseless, or otherwise hurting? Draw a line under the ones that apply.

Watch	Feel bad	Say something	Defend	Walk away
Pray	Tell someone	Comfort	Feel nothing	Talk to them
Laugh at them	Gossip about them	Offer friendship	Blame them	
Help if it wasn't too hard		Help even if it was hard		

Now draw a circle around the ones that describe **your** usual reaction to a person in need.

4 What are some ways you could help these people?

a. **Jami** has a fairly severe speech impediment. People can't understand her easily, so she's usually ignored. _____

b. **Tiffany's dad** is dying of cancer. She's afraid. _____

c. A **drunken man** asks you for money for a meal. _____

d. **Little Edgar** is being shoved around by "Da Bad Boyz" again. _____

5 **What do you think?**

A strong, single young man who refuses to work because he can live off food stamps and rent subsidy wants to borrow some bucks. On the other hand, he wants the money so he can go visit his dying mother!

Do you give him the money? (circle one)   **YES**   **NO**

DOWN AND OUT

Topic: Helping the needy.
Biblical Basis: Psalm 82

Purpose of this Session:
The down and out include the hungry, homeless, the lonely, the misfits—anyone who doesn't fit in with the crowd. They can be found in cities, suburbs, and yes, even high schools. This TalkSheet will guide your students toward their obligation to help in some way those whom the world would rather ignore.

To Introduce the Topic:
Line five or six volunteers against one wall. All they have to do is move to the other side of the room together. Easy, except one person cannot use any portion of his or her body except one arm. He or she cannot walk or crawl, but can drag him or herself by the arm. Give no other rules or details. Give a go signal and watch what happens. Call time in thirty seconds or so.

Probably everyone made it but the person with the one good arm. Point out that the best solution would have been for the other people to carry that person to the other side of the room! Did that occur to them, or were they thinking only of themselves? Introduce the session by explaining that the discussion centers on people in need and ways your students can help them.

The Discussion:
Item #1: Discuss the words, pointing out that these are the things Christians are called to do. To defend means to protect, guard, prevent injury or destruction. To maintain means to keep, hold, support, and preserve. To rescue is to free, save, liberate, and deliver. To deliver means the same as rescue and also has the idea of transport, as in taking a weak person away from a bad situation.
Item #2: Your students should discuss not only the needy they see living in city streets, but the lonely, hurting young people that can be found in any high school.
Item #3: Discuss people's usual reactions to those in need. Ask your students to tell which words and phrases would describe how Jesus would respond.
Item #4: You can have small groups work on one or two situations each. Allow time for each to reach a consensus about what should be done. If a group thinks the drunken man should not be helped with money that he is likely to misuse, encourage your students to think more creatively; the drunken man is asking for money, but what he needs is food and other types of help.
Item #5: This one may cause some heated debate. The young man is a bum, but he has a good cause. Students may be interested to know that the Bible says people who refuse to work should not be fed (see 2 Thessalonians 3:10). However, just like the drunken man above, perhaps your students can think of ways to help the young man change his attitude.

A good thought to leave with your group is that, if there are people who should not be helped, they are few and far between. Our job as Christians is to do what we can.

To Close the Session:
Encourage your students to take seriously God's call to help those who are in need. Remind them that skid row isn't the only place the needy dwell. Challenge your group members to not just feel bad for someone who is hurting, but to have the courage to get involved in practical applications of God's love.

Outside Activities:
1. Arrange for your group to do a group service project such as help at a soup kitchen for a day, collect food for a homeless shelter, or visit a hospital.
2. Find a safe vacant lot somewhere and provide cardboard, scrap lumber and plastic tarps out of which your students can make "homes" in which they will spend the night. Allow no food and provide no assistance. Afterward, have a meeting where students can debrief their night of homelessness.

AGAPE LOVE

1 Read **Matthew 5:43-44**. Place a check mark on the scale below, indicating your opinion.

"OK, Jesus said to love our enemies. But loving our enemies is . . . "

| Never possible | Very difficult | It depends | Not hard | Always possible |

2 Here are three words in the Bible that are often translated "love": **Agape** = God's perfect love. **Eros** = Romantic love or lust. **Phileo** = Brotherly love and friendship.

Place the initial of each type of love (**A**, **E** or **P**) in the correct spaces below:

___Valentine's Day   ___Family reunion   ___Marriage

___Birthday present to sister   ___Donations to charity   ___Jesus' death on the cross

___Sharing a sandwich   ___Feeding the hungry   ___Praying for an enemy

___Forgiving an unliked person   ___Infatuation   ___Flowers for a girlfriend

___A date   ___Helping a stranger

3 Look at Matthew 5:43-44 again. Place a check on the scale below to describe the sort of love Jesus is talking about:

Action-oriented   **Feeling-oriented**
(Feelings of love not required)   (Feelings of love necessary)

4 Based on what you've learned so far, give a one-sentence definition of **agape** love, the kind with which you can love an enemy:

_____

5 Check out Psalm 103:1-18. You'll find a ton of examples of the **many ways God loves us**. List four in your own words. I know God loves me because he . . .

a. _____

b. _____

c. _____

d. _____

6 **What actions could you take** to reflect God's love in one of the following situations?

a. Christy's father just died and her mom is taking it very hard. Christy, as the oldest of four children, is doing all the cooking, cleaning and child care. This is a great thing to do, but Christy is worn out and has no free time. What could you do?

b. Herman is not well liked at school. In fact, no one goes near him. He usually smells and dresses sloppy. He needs help. What could you do?

AGAPE LOVE

Topic: God's kind of love.
Biblical Basis: Psalm 103

Purpose of this Session:
This TalkSheet will allow your students to discuss some of the differences between God's love, brotherly love, and romantic love. They will learn that it is readily possible for Christians to display God's love in concrete ways.

To Introduce the Topic:
Ask several students to describe the greatest act of love they ever witnessed. Have them name the most loving person they know. Then ask them to think of one-word descriptions for both the acts of love and the loving people they mentioned. You will probably hear terms such as selfless, giving, generous, and the like. Say something like, "These are the sort of words that describe the love we are about to discuss—God's love."

Or, pass around a good dictionary and let volunteers each read one of the several listed definitions of love. These definitions range from God's love to brotherly love to sexual intercourse. Jot these on the chalkboard. Say, "Now let's look at love from God's perspective, found in the Bible."

The Discussion:
Item #1: Your students' answers will depend on how they define the type of love Jesus was talking about. If they defined it as feeling love for an enemy, then this will be hard or impossible. If they understood it to mean acts of love or kindness, this is always possible. Point out that doing an act of love for someone, even an enemy, is simply a matter of the will. Anyone can choose to love in this way.
Item #2: Have your students vote on and discuss how emotions of love (or lack of them) are related to each item on the list. Some, like Valentine's Day, go better with such feelings. Marriage goes much better! But feeding the hungry or giving to charity can be done equally well with or without the emotion we call love. Students will see that agape love is not an emotion, but an act of the will.
Item #3: Students should now clearly understand that God's love can be applied even to enemies because feelings of warmth and the like need not be involved.
Item #4: Guide your students to see that expressing God's love means choosing to do the right thing for someone in need.
Item #5: Assign verses 1-5, 6-10, and 11-18 to different groups of kids. Have students share their results. Point out that the wonderful things that God has done for us show what agape love is all about. God does these sort of things for us even though we don't deserve them. God's acts of love also serve as an example to us of the sort of love Christians should display in a needy world.
Item #6: Draw students out on whichever situation they picked. They should be able to think of several practical acts of love, including helping Christy with the dishes and laundry, baby-sitting one night a week, teaching Herman about soaps and deodorants and making sure he washes his school clothes.

To Close the Session:
Allow students private time to think of one person they could love with the love of the Lord. Have them determine one thing they will do soon for this person.

Outside Activities:
1. Organize a "secret buddies" activity: Kids draw names from a hat, then each one does nice things anonymously for that buddy (a friendship card wedged in a school locker, a flower or donut on their school desk, etc.). Keep this going for several weeks until you throw a party during which the names can be revealed. It is best if you know who is doing what for whom, so some kids won't let down their buddies.
2. You can also try a "love raid": Get the whole group together to descend en masse on someone's house with gifts and cakes and refreshments. (Get the parents' permission first!)

With Justice for All

1 Read **Psalm 106:3**. According to this verse, **what should you do to be blessed?**

2 Read **Psalm 146:7-9**. Rewrite the passage, replacing words and phrases such as "the oppressed" and "the hungry" with your **own name** or the word **me**:

_____

_____

3 **How could you help to set right the following wrongs?** If it's too late to set them right, what could you do to help in other ways?

    a. A little kid gets shoved out of line behind you.

    b. You learn that several kids have answers to an important upcoming test.

    c. You witness someone you know shoplifting.

    d. A friend is injured by a drunk driver.

    e. Your teacher always berates the class.

4 Check one or more of the following statements that best describes your thoughts about justice:

___ **Nobody said life would be fair.**   ___ **I have experienced injustice in my own life.**
___ **I don't think much about it.**   ___ **Most injustices can't be fixed, so why try?**
___ **People should stop whining and face facts.**   ___ **I am ready to right the wrongs that I see.**
___ **Christians should fight for justice.**   ___ **I've learned some good stuff today.**

5 According to Jesus in **Luke 18:1-8**, what is the believer's secret to receiving justice?

WITH JUSTICE FOR ALL

Topic: Justice.
Biblical Basis: Psalm 106; 146

The Purpose of this Session:
Sometimes life seems so unfair. Teens especially are sensitive to the injustices they see around them. This TalkSheet attempts to tap into that sensitivity and harness it with God's call for us to "maintain justice" (Psalm 106:3).

To Introduce the Topic:
Have your students suggest some of the injustices they see around them—at school, on the news, in the home. Ask them how these unfair things make them feel. Ask them how they think God feels about them. Move into the discussion by pointing out that God blesses those who stand up for justice and who constantly do the right thing.

The Discussion:
Item #1: Be sure students understand that to be blessed means to be happy or to be in an enviable state. The verse makes it clear that your students have been called to work for justice and to set wrongs right. Ask what sort of blessings a person who practices justice might receive.
Item #2: Talk about how young people who are not physically blind can receive spiritual sight from God, be set free, and the like. Impress upon your class members the fact that God serves as the ultimate example of one who upholds justice. We should and can imitate that example.
Item #3: If you like, assign each of these to a small group. Have students discuss what the actual injustices were, who might have been hurt by them, and what could be done to help set things right. Ask your students to suggest other situations they are aware of and to brainstorm possible solutions.
Item #4: Discuss each item, allowing volunteers to share what they've checked. Point out that Christians should strive for justice even if they can't always succeed. Just enjoining the battle is a testimony to the love of God and his concern for people.
Item #5: Prayer is the most important tool in the Christian's toolbox. Encourage your students to practice talking to God habitually.

To Close the Session:
Emphasize the fact that to maintain justice is an action. It is faith on wheels. It is not enough for Christians to feel pity for people who are facing unfairness. Christians must act. As someone once said, when there is human suffering, people should not ask "Where is God in this?" as much as they should ask, "Where are the Christians in this?" We are the ones who bring God's justice and mercy to hurting people.

Outside Activities:
1. Have students form an ad hoc "Justice League". They can interview schoolmates to find out what kinds of injustices are being experienced. Your students can then discuss these and brainstorm solutions at a later meeting.
2. Have volunteers use a concordance to find the Bible's references to justice, then report back to the group at your next meeting.

NO FEAR

1 What's the difference, if any, between worry and concern?

2 Here are some problems people your age might worry about. Put a **"C"** next to the ones a person would have **some sort of control** over and an **"NC"** for **little or no control** over what happens.

_____ Death
_____ Alcoholic parents
_____ Car accident
_____ War
_____ Dating

_____ Pimples
_____ Flunking a test
_____ Breaking up
_____ Body odor
_____ Substance abuse

_____ Parents' divorce
_____ Unpopularity
_____ Parental abuse
_____ Trouble with the police
_____ Pregnancy

If problems can be prevented or dealt with in some way, why do people still worry about them?

3 If you had absolute control over the troubles above, would you still worry? Why or why not?

4 Read **Psalm 112:7-8**.

According to these verses, what does a godly person have to fear? _____

What is it that makes a godly person so confident? _____
This passage (check one or more):
_____ Tells us a godly person never has problems
_____ Tells us that God will solve all problems before any real damage is done
_____ Tells us we don't have to fear problems even when they come
_____ Says that problems will come, since it talks about triumph coming at the end

5 List three things that have really worried you during your high school days:

_____   _____   _____

Pick one or two and describe how trusting and obeying God could have either prevented these problems, solved these problems, or helped you walk through them without fear.

6 "You're the Worry Doctor." Using the thoughts found in **Romans 8:28**, **Philippians 4:6-7**, and **1 Peter 5:7**, write a "prescription" for your latest patient.

R̶x

NO FEAR

Topic: Getting free from fear.
Biblical Basis: Psalm 112

Purpose of this Session:

David wrote that a righteous man "will have no fear of bad news . . . . His heart is secure, he will have no fear" (Psalm 112:7-8). Developing a righteous trust in God helps teenagers free themselves from their common worries—fear of embarrassment, unpopularity, appearance, poor health, family problems, grades, and the like. This TalkSheet allows your class members to discuss their fears without fear and to see how trust in God can cancel worry.

To Introduce this Session:

Ask your group to suggest topics that kids their age would be most afraid to talk about. What subjects would make them the most nervous? There will be many suggestions. Thank the students for their remarks and tell them not to worry—you'll cover a lot of those topics in the future. But right now, get ready to worry, because the topic is worry.

The Discussion:

Item #1: Let your class use a dictionary if you have one handy. To be worried speaks of negative emotions such as anxiety and fretfulness. To be concerned can also mean that, but it has a more positive meaning: to be responsible for or interested in something. Adam was put in charge of the garden of Eden. That was his concern—but it didn't worry him. Tell your group that it is often proper and healthy to show caring concern over problems or situations, but worry is unnecessary when we know God is in control.

Item #2: Your students will discover that many problems can be either prevented or resolved by the person or persons involved. But problems still happen—and often! That's because people don't always think or behave wisely.

Item #3: Point out that God is the only one in total control of everything. Students may ask why God allows problems to come if he's in control. He has his reasons, some of which are beyond knowing. Others include his desire to lead us to repentance and his long-term approach to history (he will set everything straight eventually).

Item #4: Problems do come to everyone. The worst can do real and lasting damage. Yet victory is in store for the Christian because ultimately God will lead us in triumph. Some problems will be handled in this lifetime; some will be swept away only when Jesus returns. In the end, all will be gone.

Item #5: Have willing students share their answers. Discuss practical steps that could have prevented or resolved each problem, then focus on how God loves each of us and is there to help us walk through problems that we either would not or could not control.

Item #6: Encourage students to remember the truths of these passages the next time they are worried.

To Close the Session:

Tell your group to take seriously the fact that God wants to drive fear from their lives. Challenge them to be people who trust in God and obey his commands. Tell them that the Bible has practical advice for dealing with specific problems. Offer to make yourself available to listen and help. Often, just talking about a problem chases the worry away.

Outside Activity:

Take a collection large enough to buy a T-shirt at your local Christian supply store. Send one or more students to hunt the racks for a Christian shirt that expresses the idea of no fear or confidence in God. Pin the shirt to the classroom wall so everyone can be reminded of today's discussion. If you like, have students write out the passages studied today on index cards. Pin the index cards around the shirt.

PRAISE THE LORD

1 **Circle the things below that you'd do if you wanted to really praise a friend:**

Ignore	Openly admire	Flatter	Criticize
Honor	Express approval	Prize	Regard highly
Serve	Make a statue	Uplift	Tell others about

2 **WHO, WHAT, WHERE, WHEN?**

Read **Psalm 113.** How does it answer the following questions:

a. *Who* should be praising the Lord? _____

b. *What* are some reasons to praise the Lord? _____

c. *Where* should the Lord be praised? _____

d. *When* should the Lord be praised? _____

3 Complete this thought: Christy reads her Bible because she wants to learn about God and life. John prays because he seeks God's help. James praises God because . . ._____

_____

4 Check your favorite two or three responses under each heading below:

What God Has Done For Me:	**What God Is Doing Around The World:**	**The Great Things I Like About God:**
__Saved me	__Keeping the world going	__His love
__Died for me	__Building the Church	__His justice
__Given me a good life	__Miracles	__His greatness
__Forgiven me	__Answering prayers	__His creativity
__Listened to me	__Saving my friends	__His eternity

5 **Write a short prayer of praise to the Lord:**

PRAISE THE LORD

Topic: Giving God praise.
Biblical Basis: Psalm 113

Purpose of this Session:

Not only is it proper for a teen to praise God, it's healthy. To focus on God's greatness is to be forced out of one's "everything revolves around me" attitude. A person focused on God's awesome nature is developing humility. This TalkSheet lets your students take a look at praise and its benefits.

To Introduce the Topic:

One reason we praise God is because he is so much greater than we are. We are nothing compared to God.

To bring this idea into the discussion, sneak into class a pinup poster of an incredibly muscular guy from one of those steroid-soaked muscle magazines. Let a few volunteer students compare muscles to each other or arm wrestle, until one emerges as "top muscle." Then show everyone the poster. Let students shout out what they think would happen if their "top muscle" met the guy in the magazine—no comparison!

There is a much greater gulf between ourselves and God. He deserves to be praised and honored.

The Discussion:

Item #1: Make a master list of students' responses to praising God. Define each item on the list. Display the list in case you wish to refer to it.

Item #2: Guide your students to understand that all believers (called servants in the psalm) are to be involved in praising God.

Item #3: Unlike prayer and Bible study (which often have tangible results), praising God can seem more abstract. At first, it may be hard for your students to answer why James praises God. There are healthy benefits, however. Your students may suggest things like these: Praise pleases God and he responds in love; the act of focusing on God is spiritually healthy; praising God helps us to understand his wonderful attributes; it's refreshingly humbling to admire God; it's exciting to realize just how great our God is.

Item #4: Conduct a poll to find out which of the listed things are most popular in your class. Ask your students to give additional examples of the things they most appreciate about God.

Item #5: Students can work together in small groups to come up with a prayer of praise. Let each group share its prayer with the class. You may wish to write a "master prayer" on the chalkboard that incorporates the thoughts expressed in each prayer.

To Close the Session:

Encourage everyone to jot down the "master prayer" and to use it as a framework of praise to God each day during the coming week. Remind your class of the advantages of praising God.

Lead in a closing song of praise.

Outside Activities:

1. Have students keep a journal of their daily experiences in praise. As they employ their "master prayer," they may discover additional reasons to praise God. Have everyone report back to the group at your next meeting.

2. Ask students to write songs or poems of praise.

idLe idoLs

1 **Check any items below that seem to be very important to the majority of people you know** (add any items you think we missed). Pick the top three to put in the target, with the bull's-eye being the most important.

_____Money
_____Making new friends
_____What others think of me
_____Popularity (lots of friends)
_____Grades
_____Fashion
_____Looks
_____Developing talents
_____Healthy living
_____Nice car
_____Partying
_____Being in love
_____Others: _____

2 **How can you know when something is a high priority?** Take the item from the bull's-eye and rate how it's regarded using the chart below:

	Lots	So-so	Never
Amount of time spent with/on it:	____	____	____
Fall down and worship it:	____	____	____
Think or daydream about it:	____	____	____
Work to get it or keep it:	____	____	____
Tell others about it:	____	____	____

3 Read **Psalm 115:2-8** and answer this question:

In Psalm 115, the people who worship idols strike me as being _____.

Give a reason for your answer.

4 Read **Matthew 6:21**. Paraphrase it, using the words priorities and worship as talked about above.

5 5. What important lessons regarding priorities and worship can you learn from **Exodus 20:3-4** and **Matthew 22:37**?

ѕLE IDOLS

Topic: Putting God first.
Biblical Basis: Psalm 115

Purpose of this Session:

The real teen idols aren't rock stars. Instead, they are whatever things take priority over God, anything that tends to shove God out of the picture. Jesus said, "For where your treasure is, there your heart will be also" (Matthew 6:21). His words explain the age-old problem of idol worship: Our hearts belong to whatever we most highly value. This TalkSheet will challenge your students to examine their priorities in light of the psalmist's comparison of the living God and dead idols.

To Introduce the Topic:

Ask your students to try to reconstruct the lyrics to the theme from the TV series *Gilligan's Island.* Tell them to imagine they are one of the castaways with Gilligan, the Skipper, the Professor, and all the rest. One day they find a treasure chest. Inside, they discover a favorite object.

Let students suggest what they would most like to find in that treasure chest. Some might suggest musical instruments, cars, swimming pools, TVs, or the like. Point out that these things were picked because they are of high priority to the owners. Lead into the first question of the TalkSheet.

The Discussion:

Item #1: In order to get an idea of the group's values and priorities, have willing students show what they've written on the targets. Have a vote to see what priorities are most common.
Item #2: Few teenagers "fall down and worship" things like money or popularity. But the discussion centered on this step can show that teenagers do spend a lot of time, effort, and thinking on their "treasures". This is the modern form of worshipping idols.
Item #3: Students may answer the question with anything from "idiotic" to "superstitious." Help them see the foolishness of valuing things over God. Verse 8 is helpful here, where the implication is that people who place their trust in things will eventually wind up with nothing—spiritually dead, unfeeling, and blind.
Item #4: This passage will help your students understand that anything that takes priority over God takes a person's heart away from God. Let them discuss the priorities from Item #1, debating whether these things are a real danger to the average person's relationship with God.
Item #5: Ask for any insights gained from these passages.

To Close the Session:

Emphasize the fact that God is looking for young people who are willing to put him first in their lives. With them, God can do mighty things. Talk about the things Christian kids should be doing to make God the Lord of their lives. Encourage them to take small steps toward God, getting in the habit of putting him first.

Outside Activity:

Have students poll their schoolmates, seeking to learn where God fits on the list of priorities in their lives.

WHY DOES GOD ALLOW SUFFERING?

 List **three tragedies** or **ongoing suffering** friends of yours have experienced:

_____ _____ _____

 Why do some people suffer or experience tragedies? _____

_____

 Why do you suppose God doesn't get rid of all suffering on earth? Pick one or more.

__ He is punishing people.
__ He is trying to get our attention.
__ He can't.
__ He doesn't care.
__ He doesn't feel suffering as we do.

__ He is trying to teach us something.
__ He is trying to make us stronger.
__ He is busy doing other things.
__ He has a plan we don't understand.
__ Other: _____

4 The following is a quote from the Bible. Complete it the way you think it probably reads.

"Before I was afflicted, I _____."

 Read the following passages and check out the *reasons why people suffer*.

Psalm 119:67, the verse you just worked on. What is the reason for the man's suffering?

John 9:1-3. What was the reason Jesus gave for the man's suffering?

John 19:1-3. Who was causing the suffering here?

Genesis 3:17-19. What is the reason God gives for humanity's suffering?

Job 1:8-12. What is the reason Job suffered?

 Read **2 Corinthians 1:3-4**. What does God do for us when we must go through suffering?

WHY DOES GOD ALLOW SUFFERING?

Topic: Evil in the world.
Biblical Basis: Psalm 119

Purpose of this Session:
Why does God allow suffering? That's a tough one, especially when he allows it to happen to us. The Bible does contain some answers and lots of comfort, as your students will see.

To Introduce the Topic:
Bring in some newspaper and magazine articles to your group that describe tragedy and suffering. Tell your students that the discussion is about suffering—why God permits it and how to find comfort in the midst of suffering.

The Discussion:
Item #1: Tragedies and sorrows are fairly common, even in high school. Allow your students to express any tragedies they have personally faced and the emotions they experienced. List the students' responses on the chalkboard for use later in the session.
Item #2: This exercise allows students to speculate about the reasons for suffering. This may be the first time some have wrestled with this question. Tell your group that, while it is often difficult to explain why a specific person is suffering, the Bible does give general reasons for the world's sufferings. Some of those reasons will be discussed in this session.
Item #3: In the exercise above, students may have realized that some suffering is the direct result of human action and some seems to be beyond human control. This item focuses on God's part of the equation, the things beyond our control (some illnesses and injuries, natural disasters, and the like). As students discuss each item on the list, be sure they understand that God really does care and that he understands suffering, because Jesus suffered so much. The following exercises lead to some of the Bible's reasons for suffering.
Item #4: If you are asked to specify what affliction was being suffered, say that it could have been long-term illness, poverty, depression, physical or spiritual attacks, or anything that caused prolonged suffering. As students work on their responses, encourage them to think of any positive results that may come from suffering.
Item #5: Assign one passage to each small group or to individuals, then have the class discuss them all. The reason the author of Psalm 119 suffered was to cause him to turn back to God. The blind man went through his suffering in order that he and others could see God's power at work. Jesus suffered at the hands of evil men. Adam and Eve and all of humanity suffer because of disobedience. Job suffered because Satan was permitted to challenge him. Thus we see that suffering can come from God, from ourselves, from others, and from Satan.
Item #6: God comforts those who turn to him. That does not mean that he immediately takes our problems away. It means he helps us walk through our troubles. Ask your students how God might have been able to help in the situations they discussed in Item #1.

To Close the Session:
Review the reasons people suffer: God is doing something or trying to teach us something; Satan is fighting us; the sins of others are affecting us; our own sins are causing us problems. Instruct your group to ask themselves the source of their problems when they do experience pain. If the source is their own sin, then they need to stop doing wrong and start doing right. If it is the sins of others, they may be able to avoid their troubles by moving in a different direction. Whatever the case, they need to draw toward God for his comfort. Discuss ways your students can draw nearer to God.

Outside Activity:
Have students brainstorm an imaginary world where there is no suffering but there are people who don't know God. What would be the advantages of such a place? What would be the disadvantages? Have your students bring in their results and discuss at your next meeting.

SOUL POLLUTION

1 Name four things that you think really pollute teenagers' minds and souls:

_____

_____

_____

_____

2 Who do you think should decide what is pollution for you?

__Parents   __Yourself   __The government
__Church leaders   __Friends

3 Read **Psalm 119:9-11**.

What was the question?	How was it answered?	What does it mean?

4 A friend of yours has just become a Christian. He or she has been involved in the four soul polluting things you listed above. Your friend doesn't want to become a hermit, but he or she doesn't want to be polluted, either. *What practical suggestions can you give your friend?*

5 Rate yourself:

The amount of time I spend doing what Psalm 119:9-11 says is enough to counter this much soul pollution in my life:

|_____|_____|_____|_____|_____|_____|_____|
Zip   Maybe a fourth   Half   Most of it   Doing Great

SOUL POLLUTION

Topic: Keeping a pure heart.
Biblical Basis: Psalm 119

Purpose of this Session:
Teens who spend two or three hours at church each week are bombarded the rest of their waking hours with pollution—spiritual pollution. The psalmist asked a question that is still essential today: "How can a young man keep his way pure?" To block the world's stain, Psalm 119:9-11 tells us to live according to God's word, seek and obey God, and take his instructions to heart. It is not possible for teens to avoid everything the world throws at them, but they can learn to be selective and careful about what they allow into their minds and hearts.

To Introduce the Topic:
Talk about the worst things your kids have ever found in their food—bugs, hair, rubbish. What did they do when they found these things? Point out that there are many things in this world that can pollute our minds and souls. It's up to us as Christians to filter these things out.

The Discussion:
Item #1: Discuss the various things your students have identified as pollutants. Which items have the potential for the most damage? Point out that some polluters are subtle and not at all obvious. Drug addiction is an obvious hazard, but television probably separates more families, robbing time that could be spent building strong relationships between family members.
Item #2: The ultimate authority for deciding what is soul pollution and what isn't is the Word of God. Parents and church leaders have a role in giving direction and wisdom. Godly advisors are qualified advisors.
Item #3: The passage reveals that God's Word is the best defense against pollution. Talk about the reasons why a heart centered on God is likely to be pure.
Item #4: As students relate what they've considered, talk about the need to be self-monitoring and discerning. What we see, hear, and partake in is up to us. The Bible is full of wisdom on which direction to go.
Item #5: Very few Christians would be audacious enough to claim that they read and meditate on God's Word enough to filter out all pollution. Yet the Christian life is one of growth. Encourage your students to move up at least one step on their rating scale. They can do this by reading the Bible regularly, obeying what it says more often, coming more regularly to youth group studies consistantly, and the like.

To Close the Session:
Help students understand that it is their responsibility to keep themselves spiritually pure. Not everything in the secular world is off-limits or can be avoided, but your learners must develop the wisdom to know what has potential to damage their walk with God.

Outside Activities:
   1. Students can work together to develop a "Soul Pollution Rating System" for movies, songs, TV shows and the like. Over a period of a week or two, they can rate popular examples of these things giving them a "Pollution Factor."
   2. Assign Psalm 119, or sections of it, to students. They are to report favorite "pollution fighters" found there.

I COUNT!

1 Here are some items that have potential. Name one way each could live up to its potential:

The *electricity* in an empty lamp socket _____

Gasoline in a gallon can _____

A *piano* _____

A *child* _____

Now write a short definition of *potential:* _____

2 Read Psalm 127.

   a. Verse 1 talks about a house and a city, which represent *a family and a community of people.* What do you think this verse is saying about families and communities that make God a priority?

   b. Verse 2 speaks of *toiling in vain without God.* What do you think this verse is saying about how to find purpose in work?

   c. Verses 3-5 center on the *value of children to a family.* What lessons do we learn about kids in each of the three verses?

3 Rate with an **X** how much you feel a person's meaning in life goes up when God is involved:

Can make a person's life worse	**No difference—people don't need God for meaning**	**Adds meaning only for those who become missionaries or pastors**	**Without God there is no real meaning in life**

4 Check one or more of the following statements that best describes your thoughts about how meaningful and full of potential your life is:

a. ___ My life is meaningless and boring.

b. ___ I'm trying to find meaning.

c. ___ The closer I get to God, the more my life counts.

d. ___ God, you can give my life meaning!

e. ___ I expect to have meaning once I'm on my own.

f. ___ There's no such thing as meaning.

g. ___ I have a lot of potential, but for what?

h. ___ I'll never be great.

i. ___ I strive to be the best I can be in life.

j. ___ I'll trust God to help me.

5 Let's say you've written a letter to God asking him to help you live up to your true potential and to lead a meaning-filled life. What do you think God would write back?

Dear

Sincerely, God

I COUNT!

Topic: Making our lives count.
Biblical Basis: Psalm 127

The Purpose of this Session:
Your students are young lives under construction, like the house mentioned in Psalm 127:1. Each student's building project will last if his or her life is built on the foundation of God by Jesus the carpenter. This TalkSheet underscores the need to wisely construct our lives according to the will of God.

To Introduce the Topic:
Write on the chalkboard or poster paper, "The best way to make my life count would be to _____."
Allow students to suggest answers, or have them write answers on slips of paper that you collect and read. Tell your group that today's topic is meaning and purpose in life.

The Discussion:
Item #1: Point out that, while everything has potential of some kind (electricity can light up a room, the piano can be played by a master), it takes effort to be realized. Potential is something that can develop or become actual; in life, it is realizing significance and purpose.
Item #2: God claims that he is the one who gives meaning and purpose to life. Encourage your students not to make the mistake of excluding God from their lives.
Item #3: Some students may feel that a person's life is meaningful in godly terms only if they are in full-time Christian service. Point out that everyone, including young people in high school, lead lives of genuine purpose and significance when they live for God.
Item #4: Encourage everyone to realize that faith is sometimes required to see the importance of our lives. Remind them of Gideon, who was a weak man when the angel of the Lord called him a "mighty warrior" (see Judges 6). He wasn't a warrior yet, but he soon would be. In the same way, we can be assured that, while we may not see ourselves as important in God's plans now, we will be able to look back at our meaningful lives someday—if we stick close to the Lord.
Item #5: Ask for volunteers to share their letters. Discuss ways your kids can grow close to God: a commitment to prayer, Bible reading, fellowship with other believers, and so on.

To Close the Session:
Have students suggest what they would like to hear said about themselves if a person's accomplishments were called out as he or she entered heaven (sort of a reverse obituary). Have your group describe how God figures in to all the things suggested.

Outside Activity:
Have your senior church staff help you gather the names of older men and women in the congregation who have led rich, meaningful lives for God. Have your group write to some of these people asking them to share the ways God has given their lives meaning and purpose. You should include a cover letter explaining the reason for the request.

A Small Circle of Friends

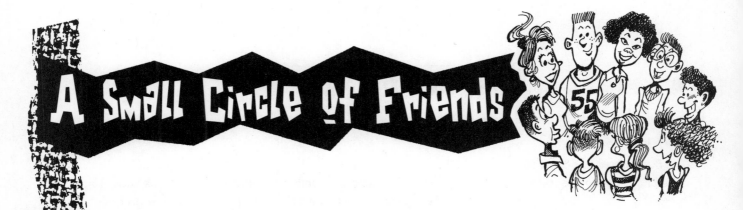

1 Name *one time you have been part of a team* or partnership that accomplished a goal:

2 Take a look at the following passages.
★ **Psalm 133:1**. What is it that's good and pleasant? _____
★ **Ecclesiastes 4:9-12**. Sum up the main idea of this passage in one sentence:
_____

3 Define Christian friendship and some of its advantages as it seems to be presented in the Bible passages you just read. Circle the words and phrases that apply.

Unity	Teamwork	Togetherness	Independent
Uniformity	Same goals	Clique	Encouragement
Hard work	Competition	Friendship	Partnership
Sincerity			

4 How could friends working together in unity help in the following situations?
A kid at school asks you to answer some tough questions about God.

A new kid in school is being bullied a lot.

A friend has an illness, possibly fatal.

5 Let's say the people you are with right now are a team. **Rate, on a scale of 1 to 10** (10 being the best), **how things are going:**

a. Our group really is a team. We work together well. 1 2 3 4 5 6 7 8 9 10
b. I feel that I am an important part of this team. 1 2 3 4 5 6 7 8 9 10
c. Our team would be willing to do something important. 1 2 3 4 5 6 7 8 9 10

Date Used: _____ Group: _____

A SMALL CIRCLE OF FRIENDS

Topic: Christian friendship.
Biblical Basis: Psalm 133

The Purpose of this Session:
What is Christian friendship? We'll define it as friendship with unity and purpose. Your teens know what friendship is. Do they know that, together as a group, they are strong and can accomplish a great deal of good? This TalkSheet deals with things that united Christian teens can do that will make an impact in the lives of others.

To Introduce the Topic:
The last part of Ecclesiastes 4:12 says, "A cord of three strands is not easily broken." Read the sentence to your students and let them explain what important lesson or lessons they think it teaches. You can demonstrate the passage graphically by challenging a volunteer to break a thread wrapped around his or her two fingers. It's easy if the thread is wrapped around once but difficult if wrapped around several times.

The Discussion:
Item #1: Encourage your students to describe in a fair amount of detail the teamwork experience; feelings, successes, and the like. Ask, "Could you have accomplished the goal alone as easily, or at all?"
Item #2: Point out that the term "brothers" in Psalm 133 is synonymous with friends and family. The advantages of teamwork, summed up in a short sentence, are: People working together accomplish more and can help each other when the going gets tough.
Item #3: Come up with a consensus of opinion and write it on the chalkboard. You might ask students who described their teamwork activities at the beginning to tell which of these things were part of their experiences.
Item #4: Guide the students to plug the words they just chose into the various situations. Come up with practical things that a group of young Christian friends would be willing to do.
Item #5: Your students may perceive themselves as anything from totally splintered to a tight-knit group of dynamic disciples. Whatever the case, choosing a good job that requires teamwork (as suggested below) will help to bond your group into a "family" that reaches out beyond itself. You may wish to collect the TalkSheets to help you uncover how the students feel about the group. Tell them in advance not to sign the sheets.

To Close the Session:
Brainstorm areas of need that your student "team" could work to fulfill. In addition to activities you are already doing (learning about God together, growing in Christ, building Christian friendships, and the like), you may be able to raise funds for a worthy cause, pick several people at school to evangelize, help a shut-in, or organize a church workday. If your group is new or otherwise not close-knit, pick an easy job like washing cars or planning an all-church softball game.

Outside Activity:
Pick one or two of the above goals that your students can reach for as a team. Organize the team into smaller groups responsible for various aspects of reaching the goal, including a group that prays. Keep track of the effectiveness of your team as it seeks to reach whatever goal or goals it has selected.

WHO DO YOU THINK YOU ARE?

1 **"Who does he think he is?"** This question would probably be most often asked at your school because (pick one):

   a. Students tend to suffer amnesia. ("Who does she **THINK** she is?")
   b. Students sometimes get their ID cards mixed up. ("Who does **SHE** think she is?")
   c. Some students believe they are Napoleon. ("**WHO** does he think he is?")
   d. Some students arrogantly treat others badly. ("**WHO DOES HE THINK HE IS?**")

2 In your experience, **conceited** people are usually (check those that apply):

   ___ No better than others   ___ Fooling themselves   ___ To be envied
   ___ In need of deflation   ___ Well-liked by others   ___ Really nice to losers
   ___ Glued to the mirror   ___ Well-liked by themselves   ___ Grudgingly admired
   ___ Easy to get to know   ___ Good listeners   ___ Interested in you

3 Take a gander at these verses to see what they teach about pride:

   Psalm 138:6. **God's attitude toward pride:** _____

   Proverbs 16:18. **The eventual results of pride:** _____

   Romans 12:3. **What prideful people think:** _____

   Galatians 6:3. **What prideful people do:** _____

4 To get an accurate picture of yourself, you should (circle one or more):

   a. Trust your inner instincts
   b. Ignore what other people say
   c. Pray that God gives you sound judgment
   d. Ask people for their honest criticism

   e. Compare yourself to famous people
   f. Use a camera
   g. Realize your worth comes from Christ
   h. Read the Bible to see how you measure up to God's standards

5 What do you think?

   "When it comes to pride, I think I _____."

WHO DO YOU THINK YOU ARE?

Topic: Conceit.
Biblical Basis: Psalm 138

The Purpose of this Session:
Conceit. Teenagers ridicule conceited people and most would probably deny they suffer from it. But conceit can show itself in many forms, including cliques, an unwillingness to do work that is "beneath" one, argumentiveness, and—worst of all—a lack of interest in God. This TalkSheet will help students discover the dangers of conceit and what to do about it.

To Introduce the Topic:
Have a student who is a good actor pantomime an expression of conceit. Let your students guess what they see. It won't be hard for them to guess. When they do, ask everyone to describe what emotional responses they have to conceit. No one likes conceit. Explain that this discussion centers on the dangers of conceit and what can be done to avoid it.

The Discussion:
Item #1: Use this tongue-in-cheek exercise to lead into a discussion of pride. What is pride and arrogance? Is it a major problem or a small one? Point out that pride can not only destroy friendships, it can cause a rift between a person and God.

Item #2: As students discuss each point, bring up other problem areas such as social exclusiveness, unwillingness to do simple or menial tasks, selfishness, and disregard for God.

Item #3: The Bible makes it clear that pride is a big problem. It angers God, leads to destruction, and involves poor judgment and self-deception.

Item #4: As you instruct your group to work on this assignment, tell them that Romans 12:3 gives a key to curing our own pride: "Do not think of yourself more highly than you ought, but rather think of yourself with sober judgment." In other words, we need to evaluate ourselves accurately.

The students' answers should lead them to understand that it is wise to listen to the opinions of other people and that a healthy relationship with God is the best bet of all.

Item #5: This exercise gives students a chance to evaluate their "pride quotient." Some may come up with a positive response such as, "I think I have no problem." Others may feel that they need help in this area. If you ask students to disclose their answers, do so only on a volunteer basis.

To Close the Session:
Emphasize that, while pride is sin, sins are forgivable. We all fail, but we know God stands ready to forgive us when we confess our sins.

Challenge your kids to behave in ways that would please Jesus. Christians should set an example for the non-Christians in the community. Brainstorm ways to combat pride in their own lives.

Outside Activity:
Devise a "Humility Exercise Chart" that features good things humble people would do. Be sure students understand that humble doesn't mean wimpy and humility has nothing to do with humiliation as the word is commonly understood. Examples of items that could be on the chart are: "Cheerfully do a yucky job at home"; "Correct an exaggerated story you recently told about yourself"; "Build up another person"; and "Make friends with an underclassman." Students can spend a week or two practicing the items on the chart.

well made

1

What do you think God thinks of these issues?

Abortion: _____

Suicide: _____

Mercy killing: _____

Murder: _____
Does he allow any exceptions to his outlook on each? Why or why not?

2

Read **Psalm 139:13-16**.

In verse **13**, what part does God take in a person's birth and life?

In verse **14**, how does the author "rate" God's part in a person's birth and life?

In verses **15** and **16**, how carefully was God watching over David's early development?

In verse **16**, what clue do we find that God carefully watches over all the days of our lives?

What do these truths tell you about the value that God places on every person?

3

Read **Romans 5:8**. What price did God and Jesus pay in order to save our lives? What does this tell you about the value God places on every person?_____
_____

4

What do you think:
a. People don't listen to Christians when we talk about   ___ Yes   ___No
   the holiness of human life
b. Society is moving toward a greater respect for life   ___ Yes   ___No
c. Higher education helps a person gain respect for life   ___ Yes   ___No
d. I can't do anything to help give value to human life   ___ Yes   ___No

5

List ways you could show respect for human life:

I could help a person in a wheelchair by: _____

I could help a person get closer to God by: _____

I could stand up for this important truth: _____

6

On a scale of 1 to 10 (10 being best), circle which number indicates *how well you think you are doing in showing respect for human life:*

1   2   3   4   5   6   7   8   9   10

Now pick the number that shows how well you would like to do. _____

WELL MADE

Topic: The holiness of human life.
Biblical Basis: Psalm 139

Purpose of this Session:

In our society, life seems so cheap—abortion, assisted suicide, murder, the unwanted homeless. But God places a supreme value on each life. That value is the suffering and death of Jesus Christ. God's plan for each valuable life starts long before conception and his plan is good. Use this TalkSheet to discuss the Christian responsibility to uphold respect for the life God has given each person.

To Introduce the Topic:

Write the words "Holiness of Life" on the chalkboard or poster paper. Ask your students to define what they think the phrase means. Have them give examples from TV, movies, public policy, school, and the like that reflect either positive or negative views of the holiness of life.

The Discussion:

Item #1: These are emotional topics that may get your students deeply involved in discussion. Although your students may not be able to reach a consensus, make sure they understand the main point of this exercise: God does have an outlook on the holiness of human life, and Christians should uphold it as best as we are able to understand it.

Item #2: Discuss what the passage has to say about God's involvement in birth and life. Your students should realize that God's involvement shows that he considers each of us to be valuable.

Item #3: The fact that Christ died for all Christians and indeed for all people (see 1 John 2:2) shows that the Lord values us more than we could have ever dreamed of or hoped for.

Item #4: These are interesting questions. Each may lead to further discussion. Stop and deal with each as time permits. Sum up the discussion by pointing out that Christians must work hard and do the best they can to promote respect for life. Christians are the only ones who fully carry God's truth; the people of the world will not arrive at it on their own. Even high school students can take positive stands and influence others toward the truth.

Item #5: Students may suggest things like feeding the hungry, leading someone to God (the greatest sign of respect for life), and taking a pro-life stand. Encourage them to look at smaller issues too, such as the needs of an "ugly duckling" in school or helping someone talk through a problem. Have students list common ways high school students show disrespect for life (fighting, prejudice, advocating drug use, gossip, cliques, and the like).

Item #6: To help students see a difference between where they are and where they should be, review the disrespectful things they just talked about. Ask how many of them have done any of these in the recent past.

To Close the Session:

Discuss the attitude Christians should take towards others who seem to disregard the holiness of life. Though we may strongly disagree with them, Christians should present God's outlook the same way Jesus did: with power, but always in love.

Outside Activity:

Have students prepare a report on the State of the Holiness of Human Life in Our Country. Statistics on abortion, murder, race-motivated crimes, and the like can be culled from news magazines.

DRY INSIDE

1 Complete this sentence: **"When I feel distant from God, it's usually because . . .**

_____

_____ **"**

2 **Read Psalm 143. How was the author (David) feeling as he wrote it? Why?**

3 What do you think: A Christian who is feeling spiritually dry . . .

	YES	NO
. . . is probably committing a bad sin that makes him or her feel that way.	____	____
. . . should read the Bible, pray and go to church more.	____	____
. . . can be a solid, committed Christian without major sin in his or her life.	____	____

4 Here is a list of things that might help a person be happy. First, pick the ones you think would help a person be happy (check YES or NO). Then, by placing an X on the scale next to the ones you picked, rate how long you think the good results would last.

	YES	NO	Short time	Long time
a. **Moving to a new place to start over**	____	____	_____
b. **Making new friends**	____	____	_____
c. **Doing nice things for others as a habit**	____	____	_____
d. **Stop doing unhealthy things**	____	____	_____
e. **Praying more**	____	____	_____
f. **Going to a Christian school**	____	____	_____

5 Read **John 13:14-17**. What lesson was Jesus trying to teach his followers? What result did he promise to those who lived according to this lesson?

DRY INSIDE

Topic: Feeling spiritually dry.
Biblical Basis: Psalm 143

Purpose of this Session:
This TalkSheet lets teens know that spiritual dryness overtakes even the best of Christians. It is not a sign that God has abandoned them. Your students will discuss reasons why feelings go up and down and one important principle that can keep the number of lows to a minimum.

To Introduce the Topic:
Have students tell about the most elated and the most depressed moments of their lives. What were the causes? How did they feel? How long did the feelings last? Say something like, "It would seem that Christians should always be happy and upbeat, because we have a living relationship with Almighty God. That's exciting. Yet Christians are just like other people. Our feelings go up and down. Today we'll discuss some important facts about feelings, facts that should help us feel good."

The Discussion:
Item #1: Feeling distant from God is one example of unhappiness. Make a list of the things that tend to make your students feel distant from God. They may suggest guilty feelings over sin, an unresolved problem, unfulfilled desires, and so forth. Make it clear that there is a big difference between feeling that God is far off and his really being far off.
Item #2: David felt hopeless and depressed. He felt faint and dismayed. He felt this way because his trials were severe (v. 3) and it had been a long time since he felt good (v. 5). Also, it seems that the answers to his prayers had been long in coming (v. 7). Through it all, however, he did not feel that God was far away. He still turned to God in prayer, recognizing that God was near.
Item #3: Discuss each item in turn. Relate them to David in Psalm 143. Was he committing a sin, not praying or obeying? Was he committed to God?
Item #4: Although all these things may affect a person's feelings, most of them are short term. A new place to live soon wears thin. New friends are nice, but even they can't keep make us happy forever. The principle at work here is that, though we foolishly tend to seek positive feelings from external things, happiness and other feelings come as a result of what we do. In other words, we can expect to feel blessed if we do what God says to do to be blessed.

   Item #5 will help your students see that service ("Doing nice things for others as a habit") is a vital key to upbeat feelings, including the feeling that God is pleased and nearby.
Item #5: Make it clear that one important solution to spiritual dryness is service. Giving, caring, sharing, looking for opportunities to make others feel better—these are ways to break the blues.

To Close the Session:
Review the idea that our emotions are under our control. To illustrate this, ask students to describe the possible emotional responses a girl might have to being asked out by a guy. She could be happy (if she liked him), mad (if he was going steady with someone else), disgusted (if he was a creep), and so forth. The emotional response is up to her.

   In the same way, we have a lot of control over whether or not we are happy. Encourage your group to do the things that promote happiness, specifically service. With your students, brainstorm practical things young people can do in the home or at school to be a blessing to others.

Outside Activity:
Challenge your students to aggressively do good things for others for the next week. When you gather again, have them share their experiences and tell if their "happiness quotient" picked up.

The Seeds of Smart Living

1 Check which of the following people you would go to for advice about a problem:

___A rock star
___A college professor
___A football star
___A bag lady
___A pastor
___A friend your own age
___An older brother or sister
___A parent or adult relative
___A complete stranger
___A counselor
___A police officer
___Other: _____

2 Go to the list above and circle those that you have a high degree of respect for.

3 Suppose you were about to be ushered into the presence of God himself. Circle the words that describe what you might feel:

Curious	Playful	Upset	Joyful	Cautious	Terrified
Concerned	Respectful	Reckless	Unconcerned	Nervous	Careful
Fearful	Awestruck	Relaxed	Self-assured		

4 Read **Proverbs 1:7**. In your own words, what do you think this passage means?

_____
_____
_____

5 What do you think a person's behavior would be like if he or she took this passage seriously?

_____
_____

6 Place an X on the line to show the degree of fearful respect you have towards God:

|____|____|____|____|____|____|____|____|
Zero   **A Ton**

THE SEEDS OF SMART LIVING

Topic: Reverence for God creates wisdom.
Biblical Basis: Proverbs 1

Purpose of this Session:
"The fear of the Lord is the beginning of knowledge, but fools despise wisdom and discipline" (Proverbs 1:7). This TalkSheet is designed to help students understand the relationship between a reverential fear of God and wise choices. Kids often seek wisdom from many unwise sources. This TalkSheet session points kids to the One who can provide real answers that actually work for life's dilemmas.

To Introduce the Topic:
Ask your students to relate a time they were zapped by an electrical shock. Discuss how they got shocked, their surprise at the power of regular house current, and what they learned in relationship to electricity. (For example, don't stick the red and black wires together.) Have students talk about their respect for the power of electricity. This is a great way to tie together the concepts of God's awesome power, the kind of "fear" (respect and awe) we ought to have for him, and the wisdom to which this leads.

The Discussion:
Item #1: Have each student select at least one person he or she sees as a source of wisdom. Allow kids to explain their choices.
Item #2: See how many of the names that your students checked are one and the same with those they respect. Help your students see how wisdom and respect go hand in hand.
Item #3: Focus on the fact that, while being in God's presence is not a trivial matter, for the believer it is not a cause for terror. A healthy view of God is one that mixes awe, reverence, and respectful fear (such as the way to approach electricity after a good shock). In today's world, many people have lost a healthy fear of God. A person who respects and fears God will seek his wisdom.
Item #4: Ask for volunteers to share their paraphrases and comments.
Item #5: Help the students understand that respect for God's guidance leads to wise choices in life.
Item #6: Allow the kids to determine where they land when it comes to real respect and reverence towards God. Do not ask them to share.

To Close the Session:
Explain to your kids that God motivates us to serve him, but never in this life forces us to revere him. (In the end though, all will.) Help your students see that one mark of true godly "fear" is a genuine desire to be obedient to his will. Point out that one starts down the path of foolish living by not giving God the respect and position in his or her life that God deserves.

Outside Activity:
Have your students look around this week for other examples of things they respectfully fear as illustrations of the fear of God. For example, the ocean could be used to illustrate God's power in its vastness and overwhelming power. Ask them to be prepared to share a few of these examples at your next meeting.

The People Who
Brought You This Book...

— invite you to discover MORE valuable youth-ministry resources. —

Youth Specialties offers an assortment of books, publications, tapes, and events, all designed to encourage and train youth workers and their kids. Just return this card, and we'll send you FREE information on our products and services.

Please send me the FREE Youth Specialties Catalog and information on upcoming Youth Specialties events.

Are you: ☐ An adult youth worker   ☐ A youth

Name _____

Church/Org. _____

Address _____

City_____ State _____ Zip _____

Phone Number (_____) _____

The People Who
Brought You This Book...

— invite you to discover MORE valuable youth-ministry resources. —

Youth Specialties offers an assortment of books, publications, tapes, and events, all designed to encourage and train youth workers and their kids. Just return this card, and we'll send you FREE information on our products and services.

Please send me the FREE Youth Specialties Catalog and information on upcoming Youth Specialties events.

Are you: ☐ An adult youth worker   ☐ A youth

Name _____

Church/Org. _____

Address _____

City_____ State _____ Zip _____

Phone Number (_____) _____

Call toll-free to order:
(800) 776-8008

BUSINESS REPLY MAIL
FIRST CLASS   PERMIT NO. 16   EL CAJON, CA

POSTAGE WILL BE PAID BY ADDRESSEE

YOUTH SPECIALTIES
1224 Greenfield Dr.
El Cajon, CA 92021-9989

Il.l....l.lll....l.l...lll.l..l.l..l.l.l.....lll

Call toll-free to order:
(800) 776-8008

BUSINESS REPLY MAIL
FIRST CLASS   PERMIT NO. 16   EL CAJON, CA

POSTAGE WILL BE PAID BY ADDRESSEE

YOUTH SPECIALTIES
1224 Greenfield Dr.
El Cajon, CA 92021-9989

Il.l....l.lll....l.l...lll.l..l.l..l.l.l.....lll

Taking The Bait

1 Imagine that a bunch of space aliens were trying to lure you away from home in order to capture you. **What kind of "bait"** (food, money, stuff, people, etc.) **could they use to snag you?**

_____

2 Has someone ever said this to you? "If all your friends jumped off a cliff, would you do it too?" Would you? Of course not! But what percentage of kids your age would probably do what all the rest of their friends are doing? Circle what you think:

Chances That A Person Would Do What His or Her Friends Are Doing:

100%   90%   80%   70%   60%   50%   40%   30%   20%   10%   5%   0%

3 Read **Proverbs 1:10-19**. What if those words were said by the parents of a foolish kid? What if they were said to a wise kid? Write the response that each kid might have to his or her parents' words of caution:

Foolish Kid	Wise Kid

4 This proverb says that the people who do wrong get trapped in their own net. Can you think of some ways that people who do wrong things get tangled up in traps of their own creation?

_____

_____

_____

_____

5 Agree or disagree with the following statements:

a. A person with friends who do wrong should change friends.
   AGREE   **DISAGREE**

b. A person with friends who do wrong should try to help them do right.
   AGREE   **DISAGREE**

c. A person who hangs with friends who do wrong is likely to do those things too.
   AGREE   **DISAGREE**

TAKING THE BAIT

Topic: The lure of bad friends.
Biblical Basis: Proverbs 1

Purpose of this Session:

For most kids, friends are a powerful component in the choices that they make and the lifestyles they lead. Good friends challenge each other to goodness, bad friends bring corruption of morals. This session is designed to help students see that the enticement of bad friends can lead to a life of misery and despair.

To Introduce the Topic:

Bring in several varieties of traps and lures. Discuss how each of them works, what kind of creature each works with, what kind of bait is used, and the probability of escape from each trap.

Another introductory activity that can be fun is called "Using Your Noodle." Put dollar bills in the bait slots of several mousetraps. Set the traps. Divide into teams and give each team a few uncooked spaghetti noodles. Instruct your teams to use their noodles to retrieve the dollars without springing the traps.

The Discussion:

Item #1: Most kids know what temptations hound them. Ask kids to reveal those items. Find out if your students think others are aware of what their weak spots might be.
Item #2: Have students share their estimates. See which kids have varying opinions and their reasons for the variances. Let them defend their opinions.
Item #3: After your students have looked at these passages and commented on the possible responses from a wise kid and a foolish kid, find out how many have heard the same sort of responses coming from the mouths of friends.
Item #4: Invite as many kids as possible to respond verbally.
Item #5: This activity will help your students see how they can begin to use wisdom when it comes to the influence of friends. Discuss the difficulties in breaking off with friends who are simply not good influences. Discuss the benefits and dangers of trying to influence those friends for good.

To Close the Session:

Although many of us think we are the exception, the truth is that bad company corrupts good morals. We must be very careful in who we choose to hang out with because not all who profess to like us have our best interests in mind. God may use us to influence our friends towards good. In fact, one of the greatest things a teen can do is to draw his or her friends towards God. But we must be strong in the faith and realize our own limitations and areas of weakness in order not to be pulled into the influence of those who are doing wrong.

Outside Activity:

Challenge your group to create an event that would be of high interest to their friends and acquaintances who are heading down a troubled path—an event that might introduce them to people whose lives and words could influence them towards considering Christ, such as a Christian rock concert, a presentation by a famous Christian athlete or media personality, or the like.

SMARTY-PANTS

1 **What do you think shows how smart a person is?** List the following indicators in order of importance, with number one being the most important:

___ Grades earned in school
___ The ease with which a person learns a skill
___ What a person does with his or her knowledge
___ How few mistakes a person makes
___ IQ test scores
___ How a person gets along with others
___ How well a person does a particular job

___ How respected a person is
___ How many big words a person knows
___ How many degrees a person holds
___ How many books a person has read
___ The size of a person's brain
___ Other:_____

2 If *genius* was 100 points and *total moron* was zero, how smart do you think you are for a kid your age? _____ How many points do you think you will have by age 30? _____

3 Have you ever really thought you were right about something—and it turned out you were wrong? Describe what happened and how you felt:

_____
_____
_____
_____

4 Read **Proverbs 3:5-6**. Write down the three most important ideas stated in the passage:

_____
_____
_____

5 If you can't trust your own heart and thoughts, who or what can you trust? Circle the best answer or answers:

a. Your friends
b. Your teachers
c. No one
d. Your minister or pastor
e. God's Word, the Bible
f. The leaders of our country
g. Yourself, your feelings and thoughts

6 How does someone *acknowledge God* in all his or her ways?

Date Used_____ Group_____

SMARTY-PANTS

Topic: Trusting God rather than yourself.
Biblical Basis: Proverbs 3

Purpose of this Session:
Teenagers are beginning the process of breaking from their parents and becoming their own independent persons. Part of this process involves moving away from unquestioning trust of their parents' word toward thinking on their own. Something has to become the governing authority for the teenager, and more often than not, that governing authority is a group of friends, the tug of awakening senses, or the typically immature logic of their own thinking. Yet God wants teens and adults alike to abandon all pretension of wisdom and understanding and seek his ways. The reward for this sensible thinking is a life that remains on course.

To Introduce the Topic:
Involve your students in an exercise in "brain power." Throw out a few riddles or mind benders for them to consider. For example, tell students that they are in a house in which all four walls have a southern exposure. A bear walks by. What color is the bear? (White, for they are at the North Pole.) Or ask them NOT to think of a white bear (Once you've suggested it, not thinking of the object is almost impossible).

The Discussion:
Item #1: Explore what components equate "smartness" to your students. List the top five they suggest.
Item #2: Having a working definition of what it is to be smart, students can estimate where they are now and where they might be in the area of "smarts."
Item #3: Use this to show that all of us, no matter how brilliant we think we are, can be absolutely wrong at the very time we think we are right. Share an appropriate example from your own life.
Item #4: Discuss that the Bible clearly teaches that all the might of human thinking is not to be trusted. God alone is the only one who has the wisdom to guide our lives. Ask kids what they think could result from thinking we can figure out life on our own.
Item #5: Who can be trusted? Discuss where and how we get God's wisdom and guidance.
Item #6: Discuss what it means to acknowledge God in all areas of our lives. Talk about how what we do and say gives a message to others about God.

To Close the Session:
Summarize that no amount of human genius or understanding is safe enough to use as a map for getting through this world. God's ideas, values, and directions are what it takes to walk a safe and straight road. His words are found in the Bible.

A person who is truly smart will realize that God is smarter still, and will try to discover what he has to say about various choices facing us in life. A truly smart person will follow what God says, even if it doesn't make sense at the time.

Outside Activity:
Collect taped interviews from people who have learned the hard way that God's way of thinking makes way more sense than leaning on their own understanding. Use it to show the brilliance of a young person who learns this lesson early rather than by the folly of a brutal experience.

DO-GOODER

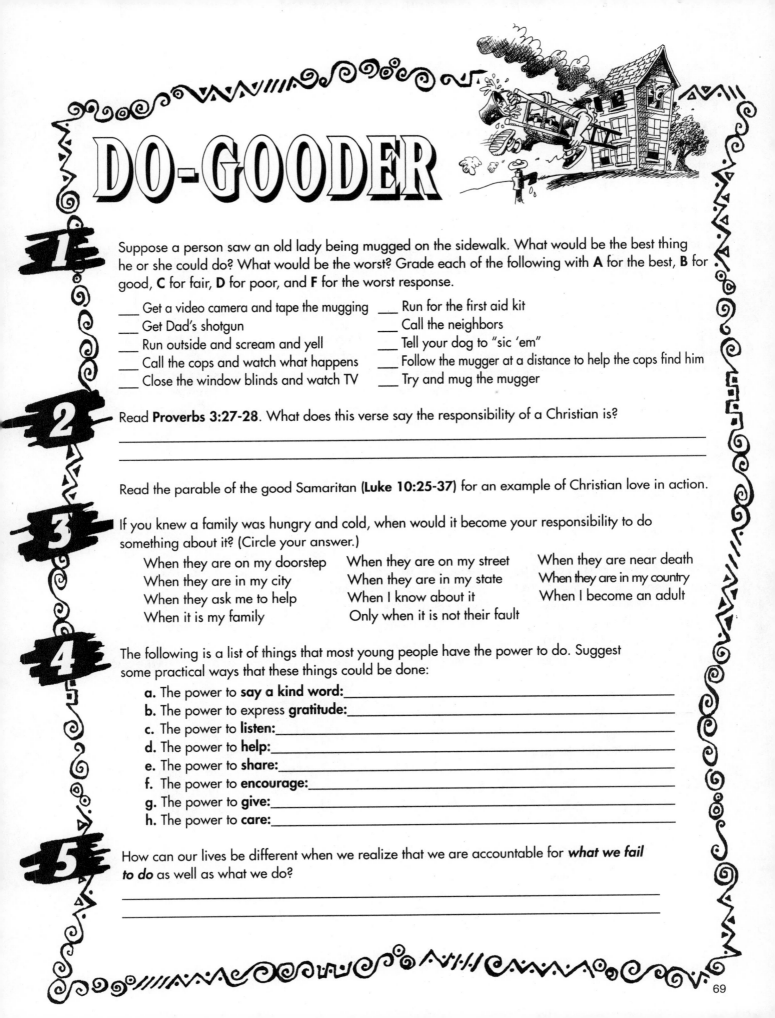

1 Suppose a person saw an old lady being mugged on the sidewalk. What would be the best thing he or she could do? What would be the worst? Grade each of the following with **A** for the best, **B** for good, **C** for fair, **D** for poor, and **F** for the worst response.

___ Get a video camera and tape the mugging   ___ Run for the first aid kit
___ Get Dad's shotgun   ___ Call the neighbors
___ Run outside and scream and yell   ___ Tell your dog to "sic 'em"
___ Call the cops and watch what happens   ___ Follow the mugger at a distance to help the cops find him
___ Close the window blinds and watch TV   ___ Try and mug the mugger

2 Read **Proverbs 3:27-28**. What does this verse say the responsibility of a Christian is?

_____
_____

Read the parable of the good Samaritan (**Luke 10:25-37**) for an example of Christian love in action.

3 If you knew a family was hungry and cold, when would it become your responsibility to do something about it? (Circle your answer.)

When they are on my doorstep   When they are on my street   When they are near death
When they are in my city   When they are in my state   When they are in my country
When they ask me to help   When I know about it   When I become an adult
When it is my family   Only when it is not their fault

4 The following is a list of things that most young people have the power to do. Suggest some practical ways that these things could be done:

    a. The power to **say a kind word:**_____
    b. The power to express **gratitude:**_____
    c. The power to **listen:**_____
    d. The power to **help:**_____
    e. The power to **share:**_____
    f. The power to **encourage:**_____
    g. The power to **give:**_____
    h. The power to **care:**_____

5 How can our lives be different when we realize that we are accountable for *what we fail to do* as well as what we do?

_____
_____

DO-GOODER

Topic: Using our power to do good.
Biblical Basis: Proverbs 3

Purpose of this Session:
Christian young people are bombarded with calls to avoid certain actions. Less frequently are they encouraged to explore ways Christians can do good to those we have the power to help. It is these acts which spell out the reality of faith to others. This TalkSheet encourages your kids to explore ideas that will stretch their faith in practical ways.

To Introduce the Topic:
Tell your kids that they are to imagine that they have become the president of the United States for one day. They have the power to do all kinds of things. Have your students contribute ideas on what they would do if they had that kind of power at their fingertips. Some kids may suggest ideas that are silly or self-serving, others may come up with ideas that are positive. The point is, all of the kids would use the power available to them for something. Let your group know that they will be discussing how they can use the power they have right now.

The Discussion:
Item #1: Ask your young people to share their grades for the various behaviors. Ask why they gave failing marks to the ones they did.
Item #2: Discuss the implications of the biblical idea that to do good when we have the opportunity is the duty and obligation of every Christian.
Item #3: Help your young people see that our obligation to help those in need is a global one. Brainstorm ways that a young person could help someone who is hungry and cold in a faraway land. Guide them to specific ideas, such as sponsoring a child through Compassion International or World Vision, or supporting church missionaries who are working in poor countries, etc.
Item #4: Give the kids a chance to discuss and explore practical ways that they might do good with the power they have at home, at school, at work, and at church.
Item #5: Help the kids summarize what changes can take place once a person begins doing all the good within his or her power.

To Close the Session:
Challenge the students to consider putting their faith into action in small but powerful ways. While we may not have people starving for food near us, we often know kids who are starving for acceptance and kindness. We can express thanks and gratitude to parents, teachers, and friends. We can serve in simple ways, by washing the church van or by helping a brother or sister with chores. We can write a letter or make a phone call that will brighten a grandparent's day. Help students discover what practical things they can do right here, right now.

Outside Activity:
Invite your students to a special day set aside to do things that are within their power to do. You could start by cleaning a portion of the church, preparing and delivering a meal for a shut-in, and other projects. Once kids experience the satisfaction that comes from this kind of service, they'll be raring for more.

Lazybones

1 How would you define laziness?_____

_____

How is **laziness** different than **relaxation**?_____

_____

2 Match each Act of Laziness with its Consequence. Put a star next to any you have experienced:

ACT OF LAZINESS	CONSEQUENCE
Late to work	Flunk class
Watch too much TV	Make a strange noise at the band concert
Don't get around to doing homework	Get a brain full of mush
Neglect to write thank-you cards	Rush to get the job done at the last minute
Don't bother to practice instrument	Grandma doesn't send you anything
Sleep in late	Miss out on much of the day
Put off doing job	Get fired

3 Read **Proverbs 6:6-11**. What does this passage suggest happens to the lazy person? What image is given of the industrious person?_____

_____

4 Your friend Arnie is in the same history class as you. Last night, your teacher gave everyone in the class a huge worksheet to fill out as homework. It took you a long time and you had to miss out on the neighborhood basketball game in order to finish the project. Arnie not only made the game, but goofed off all day long with the guys. Now he comes to you before school starts and wants to copy the answers off of your worksheet.

What Do You Do? _____

What Do You Say? _____

What Do You Feel? _____

5 What is the right amount of hours in a day for a person to be involved in each of these activities? Keep in mind there are only twenty-four hours in a day. Check the ones you think are wasteful if done too much.

___Sleep   ___Recreation   ___Watching TV   ___Hanging out with friends
___Talking on the phone ___Thinking   ___Listening to music ___Eating
___Doing chores or ___Devotions   ___Talking to parents ___Other:_____
   going to work   ___Homework   ___Reading   _____

6 **What areas do you tend to be lazy in? What could you do to make your life more fun and productive?**

LAZYBONES

Topic: Being productive.
Biblical Basis: Proverbs 6

Purpose of this Session:
Everyone has twenty-four hours in a day, yet some people seem to get a whole lot done with those hours while others barely get off the couch. One of the biblical principles to security and godliness is that of wise productivity. Young people are developing behaviors that may become the habits of a lifetime. They can learn to discipline and control their time so that they can not only work well but rest well. They can have a life that is productive, balanced, and a contribution to the world by following God's principles.

To Introduce the Topic:
On a chalkboard or poster board, write the statement, "I could get all A's in school." Line your students up and ask them to go to one side of the room if they agree with the statement, and the other side of the room if they disagree with it. Next, add to the statement by saying things like, "I could get all A's in school if I was given $50 for each A I brought home." See how many kids move to the agree side. Keep upping the money or motive (such as a new sports car) until all of the kids agree with your statement, or until you are offering $100,000 for each A.

Point out that if the motivation is high enough, almost everyone will work hard to get straight A's. The thing that keeps many of us from doing what we are capable of is our own laziness.

The Discussion:
Item #1: Ask your students to give you their ideas of what they think laziness is. Most will say that it is not a desirable trait. Discuss the difference between relaxing and being slothful.
Item #2: Discuss the results of a lazy lifestyle. Talk about how habits start when we are young and can lead to more disastrous results when we get older.
Item #3: Talk about why the ant is the biblical image of productivity.
Item #4: Discuss the situation of Arnie. Should he be bailed out? Why or why not?
Item #5: Allow your students to explore realistic amounts of time for work, play, and rest. Point out that the time they have allowed may change as they become adults with more responsibility.
Item #6: Challenge your kids to break slothful habits and to better balance their lives. Encourage them to discuss what practical things they can do to help with this process.

To Close the Session:
Encourage your students to be wise stewards of time and energy. Explain that they only have one lifetime to live; they can use it to the fullest, or squander it. Point out that while watching TV and playing video games may be fun, they are also great devourers of time with little practical return. Challenge them to pay their dues in hard work for anything from playing the guitar to getting good grades, rather than thinking they will magically get the rewards for those things in the future. As the sage said, "The worst thing in the world is a wasted life."

Outside Activity:
See how many of your students would be willing to try an experiment of giving up TV for one week. After the week, see how many were able to achieve that goal, how they used their time, and if it made a difference in how they will approach TV viewing in the future.

DISSENSION IN THE RANKS

1 **What do you think causes the most problems in a youth group?** (Check all that apply.)

___ Cliques
___ Kids who attend the group but aren't serious about God
___ Adults who are too strict
___ Boring meetings or activities
___ One or two troublemakers
___ Gossip
___ Somebody pushing strange beliefs or doctrines
___ New kids who disrupt the established pecking order

2 Complete the following sentence: **A kid who is causing problems in a youth group . . .**

3 Read the following passages of Scripture and connect each to the thought that best represents it:

Proverbs 6:16-19	There is no place for cliques among Christians.
1 Corinthians 1:10-12	Don't grumble and find fault with each other.
James 2:1-4	We should uplift other believers by what we say.
James 5:9	God is angry with those who create problems among Christians.
James 4:11	Favoritism has no room in the Christian life.

4 **What should be done in the following situations?**

Jamie does not like Sherry. Everything about her rubs Jamie the wrong way. Even though they are both Christians, Jamie takes any and every opportunity to say negative things about her. Sherry is aware that Jamie does not like her but cannot figure out why.

The jocks at First Church are nice guys individually. But together, their group is virtually impenetrable by anyone who is not part of the "in" crowd. They are such a tight group of guys that getting to be friends with them seems impossible.

Marie likes to talk. She enjoys spreading gossip among kids in the youth group. Marie is careful to never take sides. She merely acts as the conduit for all tidbits of gossip. A number of friendships have been damaged by her actions.

Arnie has been going to a meeting at another church down the road. He has come back really excited about some of the beliefs that particular church practices. He knows that the leadership at his home church does not agree with these beliefs, but he thinks they are missing the boat. Arnie is talking to other kids in the youth group, suggesting that their church is lame and that the church down the road is really into something better.

5 **What ideas do you have that could make your youth group more united?**

_____
_____
_____
_____

DISSENSION IN THE RANKS

Topic: Problems among Christians.
Biblical Basis: Proverbs 6

Purpose of this Session:
The family of God should be free from the intrigue, hurts, and meanness of the world. Unfortunately, that is often not the case. This TalkSheet focuses upon those problems that can lead to hard feelings and hurts within the body of Christ. It is a call to change for every believer who acts in ways that create pain for his or her brothers and sisters.

To Introduce the Topic:
Tell the students they are going to make up a progressive story about Christians who divide rather than unite. Begin the story by saying "Wade was new to town. He had heard from someone that the First Church had an active youth group, so . . . " then let a student proceed with the plot, continuing around the group. The only rules are that the story should be kept clean and the plot should revolve around division. Explain that today's topic deals with problems individuals in a youth group can cause the group.

The Discussion:
Item #1: Talk about what causes the most problems in a youth group. See if your group can reach a consensus on the top three trouble spots.
Item #2: Discuss your students' feelings about kids who cause trouble in the youth group. Discuss the range of motives that might cause young troublemakers to act the way they do and any solutions that come to mind.
Item #3: Talk about the ideas presented in the Scripture passages selected. Help your students see the seriousness of acting in ways that cause problems among Christians.
Item #4: Explore solutions to the various situations. See what your kids think should be done, who they think should do it, and what specifically should be said and done.
Item #5: Discuss the ideas your kids have to create a bond of love and peace among the members of your youth group. List all the suggestions given on a chalkboard or poster board.

To Close the Session:
Help your students to understand that everyone has a responsibility to keep their local church and youth group healthy, inviting, and spiritual. Emphasize that we must exercise forgiveness, kindness, and, on some occasions, discipline in order to keep the group on track. Suggest that if there are cliques operating in your group that those people learn to expand their circles of friendship. Urge kids who are at odds with one another to seek forgiveness and reconciliation.

Outside Activity:
Ask your students to come up with one thing that they could personally do to help create unity, teamwork and love among the youth group. Ask them to put that into practice in the following weeks and to keep a journal tracking the results of their efforts.

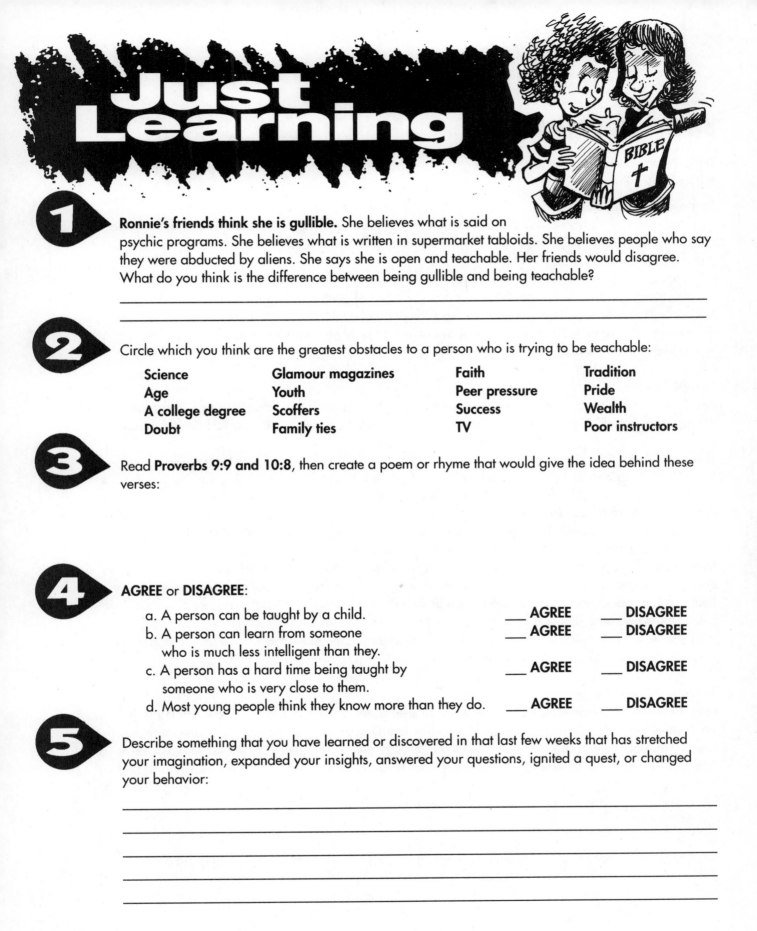

Just Learning

1 **Ronnie's friends think she is gullible.** She believes what is said on psychic programs. She believes what is written in supermarket tabloids. She believes people who say they were abducted by aliens. She says she is open and teachable. Her friends would disagree. What do you think is the difference between being gullible and being teachable?

_____

_____

2 Circle which you think are the greatest obstacles to a person who is trying to be teachable:

Science	Glamour magazines	Faith	Tradition
Age	Youth	Peer pressure	Pride
A college degree	Scoffers	Success	Wealth
Doubt	Family ties	TV	Poor instructors

3 Read **Proverbs 9:9 and 10:8**, then create a poem or rhyme that would give the idea behind these verses:

4 AGREE or DISAGREE:

a. A person can be taught by a child.   ___ AGREE   ___ DISAGREE

b. A person can learn from someone   ___ AGREE   ___ DISAGREE
who is much less intelligent than they.

c. A person has a hard time being taught by   ___ AGREE   ___ DISAGREE
someone who is very close to them.

d. Most young people think they know more than they do.   ___ AGREE   ___ DISAGREE

5 Describe something that you have learned or discovered in that last few weeks that has stretched your imagination, expanded your insights, answered your questions, ignited a quest, or changed your behavior:

_____

_____

_____

_____

_____

JUST LEARNING

Topic: Being a teachable person.
Biblical Basis: Proverbs 9; 10

Purpose of this Session:

Many parents lament about their children, "You can't tell them anything!" Their kids no longer seem teachable. Wise kids (and adults) are those who know that they don't know it all. They are those who seek out instruction and wise advice.

Teachable people are not gullible people. They think for themselves, check facts, and weigh evidence before buying an idea. Teachable folks learn from all kinds of people, young and old, simple and intelligent. They avoid the mental paralysis that comes from the pride of thinking they know it all or are somehow, because of success, grades, or brilliance, above others. Most of all, teachable people are those willing to learn God's messages and obey his commands.

To Introduce the Topic:

Ask the kids in the group to share a time when they should have read the instructions first. Share an example of your own as well. Discuss why the instructions were avoided and what you learned from the mistake.

The Discussion:

Item #1: This case study helps your kids see the difference between being teachable and being a fool. A gullible person is exploitable, easily led, and has blind faith. A teachable person wants to learn but is cautious enough to check out sources and to test truth.

Item #2: Pitfalls for those who might be teachable are many. Discuss how some of the items your students circled could be obstacles to a person who wants to be teachable.

Item #3: Explore what the two proverbs say about accepting commands and being eager to react to the wisdom shared by a godly teacher. Ask volunteers to read their poetic summations of the passage.

Item #4: Talk about where godly wisdom can be found. Discuss how and what we might be able to learn from a child or a very simple person.

Item #5: Ask group members to share what they have learned. Point out that the minute we stop learning, we begin to shrink and become more obnoxious.

To Close the Session:

Emphasize that a person must be actively trying to seek godly wisdom in order to grow and learn. Talk about the various things that teenagers can do to stimulate learning. Encourage them to read more and watch TV less. Encourage them to strike up conversations with older and more mature Christians. Advise them to be question askers and truth seekers. Tell them not to settle for a pat answer if it does not really make sense. Encourage them to seek the company of those wiser and brighter than themselves, while being alert to the voice of God speaking through children and family members.

Outside Activity:

Challenge your students to read a book that they would not normally read and then prepare a short report on the main idea of the book. Have a list of thought-provoking Christian book suggestions.

I'D BE LYING IF I SAID I WAS HONEST

1 Would you go to a doctor that you knew cheated his or her way through medical school? Why or why not?_____

_____

_____

_____

2 Circle any of the following that you would consider to be dishonest:

- Telling a caller that your mom isn't home when she just doesn't want to come to the phone
- Agreeing that a friend's dress is nice when you really think it is ugly
- Keeping the extra change accidentally given to you at the store
- Taking fruit off a neighbor's tree (who merely lets it rot) without asking
- Passing on something that is supposed to be a secret
- Taking the blame for something you didn't do in order to help another person save face
- Taking the credit for a report you copied from another source
- Saying you are going to the mall when you plan to meet someone there and then leave

3 **When you are dishonest, what do you worry about most?**

4 Read **Proverbs 10:9**. Do you agree ___ or disagree___ with the statement?
Why?_____

_____

Explain in your own words what you think the writer means: _____

_____

_____

5 Circle OFTEN, SOMETIMES, or NEVER for each of the following:

	OFTEN	SOMETIMES	NEVER
a. I cheat in school or sports	OFTEN	SOMETIMES	NEVER
b. I stretch the truth	OFTEN	SOMETIMES	NEVER
c. I trick or deceive my parents	OFTEN	SOMETIMES	NEVER
d. I keep my word and promises	OFTEN	SOMETIMES	NEVER
e. I take what is not mine to take	OFTEN	SOMETIMES	NEVER

6 Read the Scripture verses below. Then, make a list of God's standards for integrity.
Exodus 23:1; Leviticus 19:11; Psalm 37:21; Proverbs 14:5

I'D BE LYING IF I SAID I WAS HONEST

Topic: Integrity.
Biblical Basis: Proverbs 10

Purpose of this Session:
Teens face choices: Will they be true to their word? Will they cheat at sports, games, or schoolwork? Will they deceive others to get out of trouble? Will they embellish events in an attempt to increase their social stature?

God sets high standards in the area of integrity. But as high as they are, they are achievable and rewarding, especially when a life of integrity becomes a habit.

To Introduce the Topic:
A few days before the session, send out a mailing reminding students of the upcoming meeting and promising a prize for each person who brings the mailer to class. A good number will show up with mailer in hand. Pretend that you forgot about your promise, or that you changed your mind. Start your session by asking how many students are upset that you did not keep your word. Ask them if they feel they could trust you in the future. Finally, introduce your topic and then tell your students that you do have prizes that you will give out at the end of the session.

The Discussion:
Item #1: Let your kids explain why they wouldn't trust a doctor who cheated through medical school. Throw in a few more examples, such as: A president who lied to get into office, an athlete who set a world record while using illegal drugs, or a police officer who took bribes from rich crooks. Point out that honesty is one of the pillars of society because trust between people is essential for a healthy society.
Item #2: Have your group discuss why the actions listed are dishonest or not. Be prepared to discuss what could be said that could be honest, yet gentle, as in the case of the girl with the ugly dress. Allow for some disagreement here.
Item #3: Discuss the downside of dishonesty. Most liars, cheaters, promise breakers, and thieves live in fear that they will be caught. Their pulse rises when someone gets too close to the truth, or when a police car drives by.
Item #4: Talk about the value of a mind and heart at peace. Discuss the security gained in being honest.
Item #5: Without asking kids to be too revealing, see how many will concede that they struggle with honesty. Share an appropriate example of an area where you struggle to maintain integrity.
Item #6: Point out that God has definite ideas and standards for integrity. While he willingly forgives all shortcomings, he wants honesty to become the standard for our lives.

To Close the Session:
Give your students a chance to affirm their commitment to being people of integrity by creating a Pledge of Integrity document which your kids can read and sign if they are willing to try living a life of honesty. Be sure to give out the prizes that you promised!

Outside Activity:
Ask your students to attempt to keep their word for the entire week. They are not to make any promises, even small ones, unless they are willing to keep them. Assign partners to provide accountability and encouragement.

WICKED

1

What do you think? **A** = Agree   **NS** = Not Sure   **D** = Disagree

  a. The people of our generation are less wicked than past generations. ___
  b. It is unpopular to call anyone wicked nowadays. ___
  c. All people are wicked. ___
  d. Wickedness is a word that should be reserved for really, really bad people. ___
  e. People are not really wicked, just their deeds. ___
  f. I don't know anyone personally that I would consider wicked. ___
  g. Wicked people are often very nice people. ___
  h. Being wicked is romanticized in our culture. ___

2

Read **Proverbs 10:23-25, 27-30**. Now write down briefly what will happen to each of the following two people:

The Righteous Person   **The Wicked Person**

3

How do you think a person becomes wicked or righteous? Mark which responses you think are correct:

  ___ A person becomes righteous or wicked based on his or her upbringing.
  ___ The choices a person makes determines if he or she will be righteous or wicked.
  ___ A person is born one way or the other.
  ___ God makes some people righteous and some people wicked.
  ___ Wicked people are that way because they've gotten involved in the occult.
  ___ A person who gives Christ control of his or her life will be made righteous.
  ___ A person becomes wicked or righteous based on who he or she hangs out with.
  ___ A person can never be wicked or righteous; everyone is a mix of both.

4

Respond to the following questions:
  a. Is it right for Christians to declare particular actions or people as wicked?
     Yes _____ **No** _____ **Undecided** _____
  b. Is it right for Christians to attempt to stop some kinds of wickedness?
  If yes, give an example.)
     Yes _____ **No** _____ **Example** _____
  c. Is it right to use force to stop some forms of evil?
     Yes _____ **No** _____ **Undecided** _____
  d. Should Christians try to convince the wicked that they are really wicked?
     Yes _____ **No** _____ **Undecided** _____

5

What do you think is the best response towards those who are practicing wickedness?

79

WICKED

Topic: Human wickedness.
Biblical Basis: Proverbs 10

The Purpose of this Session:

Young people live in a world that has rendered certain terms as politically incorrect or archaic. Wickedness is one such term. Modern society sometimes acknowledges bad actions, but hesitates to call anyone wicked. Sickness and neurosis have replaced evil and internal wickedness as motivations for horrendous actions. Those who insist on using the ancient terms are often seen as old-fashioned or insensitive.

But wickedness is real. It lies deep in the heart of each person. The Scriptures use no velvet glove to bring out the human condition: a person in rebellion from God is wicked.

This TalkSheet session will give your kids a reality check on human wickedness.

To Introduce the Topic:

Ask your students to nominate people for the dark honor of being the most wicked human being to walk the face of the earth. Select the top five candidates and invite your kids to talk about what makes them wicked. Then, have your group vote for whom they think is the most wicked human ever to walk the earth. This activity will get your kids thinking along the lines of today's session.

The Discussion:

Item #1: Discuss with your kids the various ideas floating around about wickedness. Note that we often reserve the word wicked for the very worst of humans. In fact, many of us cannot even think of a person who we would call wicked.

Item #2: Talk about the teaching of the Bible and the eternal results of righteousness and of wickedness. Point out to your kids that a look in the mirror will show them a wicked person, in the event they cannot think of one.

Item #3: Explore how a person becomes wicked and how he or she becomes righteous. Point out the truth and error in many of the statements.

Item #4: Use these questions to discuss what a Christian's response ought to be to wickedness. Bring out the pros and cons of each question, and allow for debate and disagreement within your group.

Item #5: Talk about what each Christian can do personally to solve the problem of human wickedness.

To Close the Session:

Help students understand that there is a solution to human wickedness. That solution is Christ as the Lord and Master of each life. Point out that the way we demonstrate righteousness is to practice right actions and thinking. Note that if we do not put energy and effort into our Christian life, we will tend to drift towards wickedness. Help your students see that real wickedness is rebellion against God and not just horrible deeds committed by the worst of humans.

Outside Activity:

Ask your students to commit themselves to a five-minute period of self inspection each day for the next week. Ask them to use that time to weigh their thoughts, deeds, and choices to see if they have acted in a way that will lead them toward righteousness. Discuss the results of their efforts at your next meeting.

A RING IN A PIG'S SNOUT

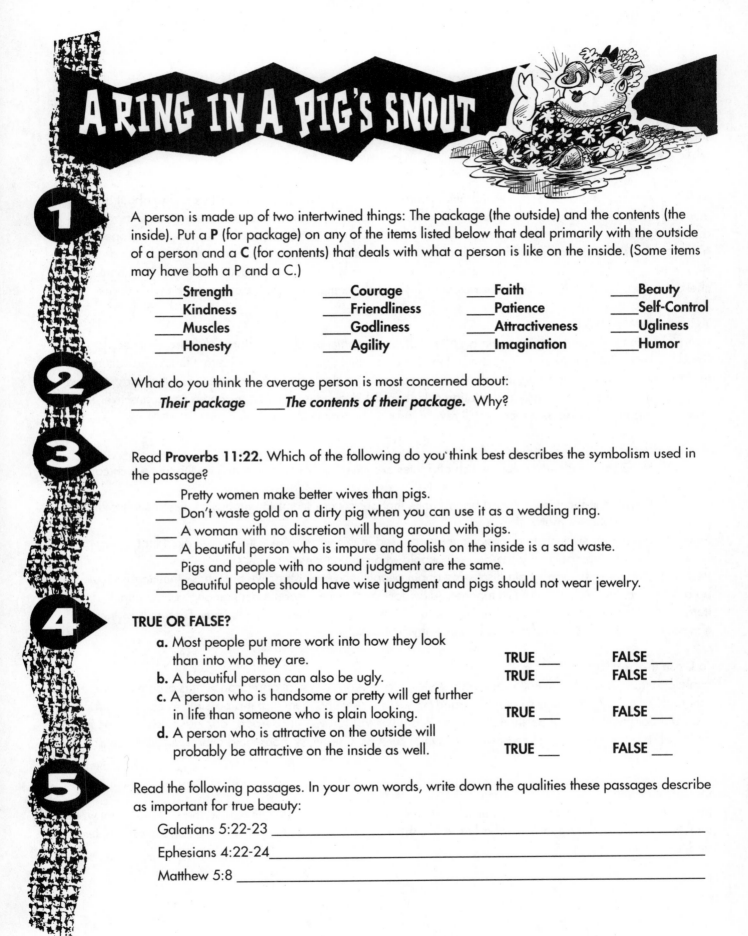

1 A person is made up of two intertwined things: The package (the outside) and the contents (the inside). Put a **P** (for package) on any of the items listed below that deal primarily with the outside of a person and a **C** (for contents) that deals with what a person is like on the inside. (Some items may have both a P and a C.)

____Strength	____Courage	____Faith	____Beauty
____Kindness	____Friendliness	____Patience	____Self-Control
____Muscles	____Godliness	____Attractiveness	____Ugliness
____Honesty	____Agility	____Imagination	____Humor

2 What do you think the average person is most concerned about:

____*Their package*   ____*The contents of their package.* Why?

3 Read **Proverbs 11:22.** Which of the following do you think best describes the symbolism used in the passage?

___ Pretty women make better wives than pigs.
___ Don't waste gold on a dirty pig when you can use it as a wedding ring.
___ A woman with no discretion will hang around with pigs.
___ A beautiful person who is impure and foolish on the inside is a sad waste.
___ Pigs and people with no sound judgment are the same.
___ Beautiful people should have wise judgment and pigs should not wear jewelry.

4 **TRUE OR FALSE?**

    a. Most people put more work into how they look
    than into who they are.   TRUE ___   FALSE ___

    b. A beautiful person can also be ugly.   TRUE ___   FALSE ___

    c. A person who is handsome or pretty will get further
    in life than someone who is plain looking.   TRUE ___   FALSE ___

    d. A person who is attractive on the outside will
    probably be attractive on the inside as well.   TRUE ___   FALSE ___

5 Read the following passages. In your own words, write down the qualities these passages describe as important for true beauty:

    Galatians 5:22-23 _____

    Ephesians 4:22-24_____

    Matthew 5:8 _____

A RING IN A PIG'S SNOUT

Topic: Inner beauty.
Biblical Basis: Proverbs 11

Purpose of this Session:
Kids know that appearance is important, and spend much of their time primping and worrying about how they look. What is often lost is the need to put at least an equal amount of time and attention in to developing an attractive inner character. It is a person who is attractive on the outside, but who has never developed the ability to make wise choices, that the writer of Proverbs equates with a pig (unclean to the Jews) with a gold ring in its nose. This TalkSheet will give you an opportunity to talk with your students about working on their character, their spiritual lives, and their personalities with the same fervor that they work on their exterior.

To Introduce the Topic:
Bring in some books and magazines (e.g., *National Geographic*) that have pictures of "attractive people" from different cultures and eras. Pass around the pictures while you note that in different times and cultures, the concept of "beauty" can vary widely. Renaissance painters show the beautiful women of their day as quite heavy by our standards; in ancient Hawaiian culture, a 300-pound man was considered very attractive. Tell your students that the discussion today will revolve around beauty, both inner and outer.

The Discussion:
Item #1: Have your students explore which attributes are external or internal in nature. Discuss which can be both.
Item #2: Discuss the focus on outward appearance that our culture seems to emphasize. Discuss what kind of problems this creates for many of us.
Item #3: Invite your students to discuss the imagery used in this verse. Make sure to point out that a pig was considered an unclean animal to the Hebrew people who created these proverbs.
Item #4: Use this quiz to stimulate discussion about people who look attractive but whose thinking is mixed up or who live their lives in a foolish manner. Allow for debate and disagreement among your group.
Item #5: Let the kids describe what the Bible says are qualities that create inner beauty. Discuss how these can get better with age, rather than fading like physical beauty.

To Close the Session:
Explain to the group that while it is important to take care of our physical appearance, it is even more important to develop our character, spiritual life, and personality. Remind them that it is possible to be an attractive fool. The body we have will be shed, but who we are will last forever. Encourage your kids to spend time in personal devotions and discipline-building activities such as Bible study, household chores, and service projects.

Outside Activity:
Invite your students to decorate their mirrors at home with Bible verses that will remind them to put equal work into their souls as they are into their bodies. Give them a list of verses that they can copy on to Post-It notes and take home.

TAKER OR GIVER?

1 **Circle the last person you gave a gift to:**

Mom	Dad	Brother	
Sister	Neighbor	Boyfriend	Aunt
Grandpa	Friend	Teacher	Minister
Girlfriend	Uncle	Grandma	Self

2 Complete these statements with the words that seem best to you:
   a. ***A generous person is likely to*** _____.
   b. ***There is giving and there is receiving. If I had a choice, I would*** _____.
   c. ***The best way to give a gift is*** _____.

3 What is one gift that you would like to give if you could afford it? Who would you give it to? Why?
   _____
   _____

4 **Check the three best ways to be a giver:**
   ___Do someone a favor   ___Lend a hand
   ___Buy something for someone   ___Put money in the church offering
   ___Send money to a third-world country   ___Visit a lonely senior citizen
   ___Say something kind to someone   ___Other: _____

5 Read **Proverbs 11:24.** What doesn't appear to make sense in this verse? What could the answer be?

6 Read the following passages. Then, rewrite them into a single poem or lyric that could be easily memorized.

   2 Corinthians 9:7   **Matthew 6:1-4**   **Acts 20:35**   **Proverbs 22:9**

TAKER OR GIVER?

Topic: Developing a generous spirit.
Biblical Basis: Proverbs 11

Purpose of this Session:
Many teens totter on the fence between childish selfishness and mature generosity. It is during this stage in life that young people will develop giving habits that will stay with them for the rest of their lives.

Giving does not mean money alone. It means actions and time. Young people can learn to give generously even when they are flat broke.

To Introduce the Topic:
Describe the following situation to your students:

"Mrs. Wyman, the elderly widow who lives down the block, will not be home this Halloween evening. She loves the neighborhood children and does not want to disappoint any of them who may come to her house to trick or treat. Mrs. Wyman buys a few bags of candy and pours them in a box outside her house. Above the box, she places a sign that says, Please take ONE."

Ask your students to vote thumbs up (yes) or thumbs down (no) on the following questions: Will the box be empty when Mrs. Wyman gets home? Will the box be empty early in the evening? Will kids respect her wishes? Should kids respect her wishes? Would you do what Mrs. Wyman did? Why or why not?

Use this example as a starting point to talk about being people who are self-centered or other-centered.

The Discussion:
Item #1: Discuss the reasons and occasions for gift giving.
Item #2: Explore various ideas your kids have about giving. Some may feel that to be generous is to be taken advantage of; others may feel that getting is more fun than giving. Discuss the fun in both giving and receiving.
Item #3: Have your students discuss who they would give their dream gift to and why. Ask how it would make them feel to be able to give such a gift.
Item #4: Explore the idea that being a giving person involves more than mere gift buying. A giver gives in all areas of life, some of which are worth much more than a tangible item.
Item #5: Discuss God's strange but functional economy: To give is to gain, to die is to live, to be last is to be first, etc. Have your kids brainstorm how these truths might apply in real-life situations.
Item #6: Have a few willing students share their poems or lyrics. Encourage them to commit their creations to memory. Discuss which of the attributes in the passages they read are most needed in life today.

To Close the Session:
Discuss the blessings and benefits that come to both the giver and receiver. Ask your group to brainstorm ideas on things that could be given, with little or no money, at home, school, or church.

Outside Activity:
Have each student select the name of one person they can be generous to during the coming week. Have them write down a journal of the "gifts" they have given, what resulted from their actions, and how the experiences made them feel. Have your kids bring their journals to the next meeting and share what happened.

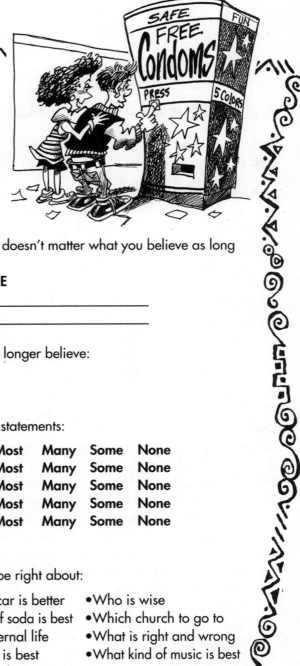

SINCERELY WRONG

1 Do you agree or disagree with the following statement: "It doesn't matter what you believe as long as you are sincere."

AGREE	**DISAGREE**
Why?_____	Why?_____
_____	_____

2 List something that you once believed was true that you no longer believe:

3 How many of your friends would agree with the following statements:

a. If it is in the paper or on TV, it must be true.	**Most**	**Many**	**Some**	**None**
b. If it makes sense to me, it must be true.	**Most**	**Many**	**Some**	**None**
c. If everyone else believes it, it must be true.	**Most**	**Many**	**Some**	**None**
d. If it is in the Bible, it must be true.	**Most**	**Many**	**Some**	**None**
e. If my parents believe it, it must be true.	**Most**	**Many**	**Some**	**None**

4 Circle the statements below that you feel are important to be right about:

- Which toothpaste gives sex appeal
- Which basketball team is best
- What friends to hang out with
- Who makes the best hamburgers
- What to do if someone is choking

- What kind of car is better
- Which brand of soda is best
- How to find eternal life
- Which college is best
- Where to put oil in a car

- Who is wise
- Which church to go to
- What is right and wrong
- What kind of music is best

5 Read the two passages below. How might each answer a person who believes that sincerity is all that matters?

Proverbs 14:12 _____

_____

John 14:6 _____

_____

SINCERELY WRONG

Topic: God's way is the only way.
Biblical Basis: Proverbs 14

Purpose of this Session:
Most young people quickly affirm that it doesn't matter what a person believes as long as he or she sincerely believes it. This faulty line of thinking produces some big problems for kids. For example, it flies in the face of Christ's words proclaiming himself to be the only source of life-giving truth (see John 14:6).
   This TalkSheet session will help your students compare the blurred thinking of the world with biblical truth.

To Introduce the Topic:
Ask your students if any know why American natives were called "Indians" by the European discoverers. It is because Columbus thought that he had landed in India. He did not at first realize he had discovered a new world. Columbus sincerely believed that these dark-skinned people were from India. Did the honest belief of Columbus really make the people he met true "Indians"?
   Use this example as a way to move into the first question on the TalkSheet.

The Discussion:
Item #1: Let the students say where they stand on the issue of sincerity being the basis for truth. Allow for a diversity of opinion at this point.
Item #2: Talk about the things students once believed (Santa Claus, the moon is made of green cheese, monsters under the bed, and so forth). Discuss what changed those beliefs and what kids think about those who hold to what they consider to be strange ideas or superstitions.
Item #3: Discuss who we tend to believe and why. Challenge kids to really think about these sources of information—are they are always accurate and reliable?
Item #4: Have a few volunteers share their answers. Talk about the things that are very important to get right. Discuss what happens to people who think they are smart enough to make their own way in life.
Item #5: Discuss the implications of these passages. What options do they give to people who want to believe whatever they think is right?

To Close the Session:
Point out that while sincerity is noble, it does not keep us from being sincerely wrong. Demonstrate to your students that the teachings of Scripture delineate good and bad, right and wrong. The Scriptures are solid even if we sometimes find their truths to be uncomfortable. Challenge your students to think carefully about the various "truths" they hear and to compare them to the Word of God.

Outside Activity:
Help your students create a Nonsense Meter. Make it out of junk electric parts and use it as a fun gimmick to pull out whenever some wild story, stupid idea, or tall tale is being discussed in your group.

SiMPLe SiMON

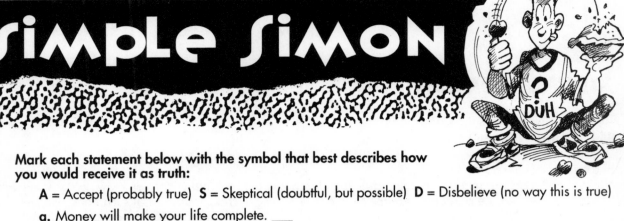

1 Mark each statement below with the symbol that best describes how you would receive it as truth:

A = Accept (probably true) **S** = Skeptical (doubtful, but possible) **D** = Disbelieve (no way this is true)

a. Money will make your life complete. ___
b. Angels regularly visit people. ___
c. Aliens from space abduct people now and then. ___
d. You are likely to be hit by lightning. ___
e. Friends are the biggest influence in the lives of kids. ___
f. Hitler was a nice guy when you got to know him. ___
g. There is a direct correlation between study and grades. ___
h. Someday all diseases will be wiped out by science. ___
i. Men have walked on the moon. ___
j. Elvis is alive. ___
k. If most people believe something to be true, then it is. ___
l. People are a lot kinder now than they were in the past. ___

2 "There's a sucker born every minute." Do you agree or disagree with this old saying?
____ **Agree**   ____ **Disagree**
Why?

3 Circle which people or things you feel only a simpleton would believe in or rely upon;

Horoscopes	Extraterrestrials	Fortune cookies	Supermarket tabloids
Human evolution	Faith healers	Psychological testing	Palm reading
TV news programs	Politicians	Talk show hosts	School textbooks
Movie stars	Ministers	Tea leaves	Rock stars
Newspapers	Teachers	Parents	Doctors
Scientists	Friends		

4 Read **Proverbs 14:15**.
What is the definition of a simple person?

What is the definition of a prudent person?

5 **What advice would you give to the following people?**
Audrey has lots of questions about Christianity. Some Christian kids have told her that she has to stop asking questions and just have faith. Others have told her that truth can stand up to investigation. Audrey comes to you with her dilemma. What would you tell her?

Dave is always coming to school with some new discovery. First he got all excited about ecology and bugged people if their book covers were not made of recycled paper. Next, he became a vegetarian and tried to have meat banned from the cafeteria. He is now eating hamburgers again but recently got into the idea that aliens have visited earth. You are running out of patience with Dave. What would you say to him?

6 What would be a wise way to deal with doubts, new information, and new ideas?

Date Used _____ Group _____

SIMPLE SIMON

Topic: Becoming a thinking Christian.
Biblical Basis: Proverbs 14

Purpose of this Session:

Millions of dollars are made from tabloids screaming about the Loch Ness monster showing up in the Great Lakes, or the kid whose parents are really Martians. Most high school kids scoff at such nonsense, yet they often swallow shallow "facts" tossed around by the current culture and the media. Kids need to learn how to thoughtfully question what they are being told. They need to wonder about the validity of what they hear and see. Since all truth can stand investigation, even questions about spiritual things are fair game.

Christians can honestly approach ideas and issues, looking for truth and sense. This TalkSheet session will encourage kids to become thinkers, to check facts, and to seek truth.

To Introduce the Topic:

Pass out slips of paper to your students. Half of the slips should be marked with an X. Those who receive marked slips should keep that information secret.

Tell your students that each is to tell an amazing fact or piece of information. However, those with an X on their papers are to invent a false "fact." A person might say, "My mom's middle name is George." The rest of the group votes about the statement—truth or lie? The person then reveals whether it is the truth or not. The goal is for the liars to be convincing enough to sway the group.

Move into the discussion by pointing out that much of life is like the game just played: People, governments, ad agencies, and others often play fast and loose with the truth.

The Discussion:

Item #1: Ask your students to share their answers. Who sees themselves as skeptics? As believers?
Item #2: Discuss the gullibility of the human race. Ask your kids to give any examples of ways they think people are suckered.
Item #3: Talk about what or who a simple-minded person would tend to trust. Have any of your learners been "fleeced" or know anyone who has?
Item #4: Discuss what it means to be simple and what it means to be prudent in God's economy. Discuss what a prudent person is like, how they would process information, and how they would decide what was true and right.
Item #5: Have volunteers share their answers. As an alternative, break your students into smaller groups and have them work on these scenarios together.
Item #6: Talk about the wise way to deal with ideas and information. Point out that it's OK for Christians to have doubts and questions about their faith, and discuss how to thoughtfully explore honest doubts.

To Close the Session:

Remind your students that their minds are a gift from God. A wise person will not blindly believe all information that comes his or her way. Point out that truth can stand investigation. Christianity is worth believing because it can be investigated. Discuss where faith comes into the picture. Mention that we tend to have faith in those who we think we can trust: a teacher, a minister, a political leader, a newsperson. Note the danger in handing over our minds to someone else. We must reserve complete trust for God alone. Let your kids know that being prudent rather than a simpleton involves mental and spiritual effort.

Outside Activity:

Ask your students to go through magazines, newspapers and ads and bring in any examples of half truths, lies, or exaggerations they find to share at your next meeting.

BIG SHOT?

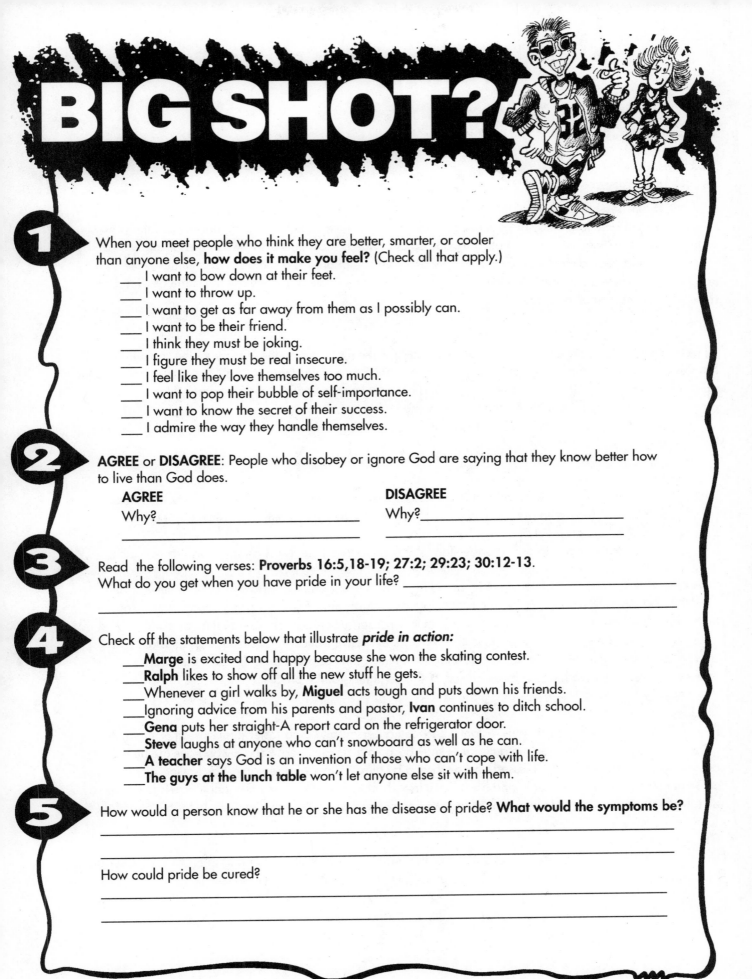

1 When you meet people who think they are better, smarter, or cooler than anyone else, **how does it make you feel?** (Check all that apply.)

___ I want to bow down at their feet.
___ I want to throw up.
___ I want to get as far away from them as I possibly can.
___ I want to be their friend.
___ I think they must be joking.
___ I figure they must be real insecure.
___ I feel like they love themselves too much.
___ I want to pop their bubble of self-importance.
___ I want to know the secret of their success.
___ I admire the way they handle themselves.

2 AGREE or DISAGREE: People who disobey or ignore God are saying that they know better how to live than God does.

AGREE
Why?_____
_____

DISAGREE
Why?_____
_____

3 Read the following verses: **Proverbs 16:5,18-19; 27:2; 29:23; 30:12-13**.
What do you get when you have pride in your life? _____
_____

4 Check off the statements below that illustrate *pride in action:*

___ **Marge** is excited and happy because she won the skating contest.
___ **Ralph** likes to show off all the new stuff he gets.
___ Whenever a girl walks by, **Miguel** acts tough and puts down his friends.
___ Ignoring advice from his parents and pastor, **Ivan** continues to ditch school.
___ **Gena** puts her straight-A report card on the refrigerator door.
___ **Steve** laughs at anyone who can't snowboard as well as he can.
___ **A teacher** says God is an invention of those who can't cope with life.
___ **The guys at the lunch table** won't let anyone else sit with them.

5 How would a person know that he or she has the disease of pride? **What would the symptoms be?**
_____
_____

How could pride be cured?
_____
_____

BIG SHOT?

Topic: Destructive pride.
Biblical Basis: Proverbs 16; 27; 29; 30

Purpose of this Session:
All young people are tainted by the disease of pride. It can surface as feelings of superiority or inferiority, bragging, fault finding, an arrogant attitude, and so on. Pride is most destructive when it challenges God.

Many young people challenge God passively. They simply ignore his commands, sometimes while professing to believe them. The cure to pride is humility—the realization that we are the same as everyone else and that we all melt before God.

To Introduce the Topic:
Have all your students stand in the center of the room. Tell them to move to the left side of the room if they have ever said to someone else, "Our car (or thing) is cooler than your car (or thing)." Have them move to the right side of the room if they have ever said, "I'm a better student (or athlete) than you are." Have them sit down if they were right. Have them stand if they were bluffing or didn't know.

Have your kids discuss why people say stuff like this. Use this as a means to begin discussing pride and how it is displayed.

The Discussion:
Item #1: Talk about how it feels to be confronted by a pride-filled person. Ask, "Do you think that these people are aware of their own pride?" Discuss the idea that some people build themselves up out of insecurity, while others do it out of arrogance.
Item #2: Help your students to define pride. Talk about the more subtle forms of pride such as resistance, stubbornness, and quiet rebellion.
Item #3: Discuss the results of sinful pride, both eternal and temporal. Ask, "How does God view pride?"
Item #4: Explore which actions are truly prideful and which are not. Allow for some debate and disagreement here. After awhile, see if your kids can come to a consensus on a working definition of pride.
Item #5: Discuss the symptoms of pride: self-obsession, excessive insecurity or arrogance, constant worry over what others think, etc. Have volunteers share what they think people can do to cure the disease of pride. Stress that a focus on God, and a focus off self, is the beginning of the process.

To Close the Session:
Explain to your group that pride puts distance between a person and God faster than any other thing. A prideful person acts as the supreme authority—they become their own god. People who have the humility to obey God are people who are blessed and rewarded by him. People who see others as having worth and value get along better with people and have more friends than those who are arrogant. Discuss how Christ dissolved the barriers of pride by eating with social outcasts and picking common people for his disciples.

Outside Activity:
Have each student in your group write out one of the proverbs studied today to hang in his or her locker or bedroom as a reminder of what his or her attitude should be towards God and others.

BLOWING YOUR STACK!

1 Think of the last time you lost your temper. What happened?

I lost my temper with: ___A brother ___A sister ___A parent
___A friend ___A teacher ___An animal
___A stranger ___A member of the opposite sex
___Other: _____

I got mad about: ___What somebody said
___What somebody did to me
___What somebody should have done but didn't
___What somebody did to someone else
___I don't remember, but it was bad
___Other: _____

2 **What is the difference between being angry and losing your temper?**

3 Rate the ways people react when they lose their temper, with one being the worst and eight not so terrible. Then put checks by the behaviors you demonstrate when you blow your stack.

_____ *Slam doors and bang around*
_____ *Scream and yell*
_____ *Get mad at people who have nothing to do with the situation*
_____ *Clench fists, grind teeth, breathe hard*
_____ *Say hurtful words*
_____ *Hit, slap, scratch, push*
_____ *Throw things, destroy property*
_____ *Use foul language*

4 Do you think a temper is a controllable thing? _____**Yes** _____ **No**
Why or why not?

5 Look up the following passages. Then, number them (with 1 being most important) in the order you think is most important for people to grasp:

___Proverbs 16:32 ___Proverbs 15:18
___Proverbs 19:19 ___James 1:19
___Proverbs 12:16 ___Ephesians 4:26
___Proverbs 15:1

6 Can you think of someone who you recently blew your stack at? Write that person's name here:_____
Would you be willing to go to this person and ask forgiveness for losing your cool?
___**Yes** ___**No**
Why or why not?_____

BLOWING YOUR STACK!

Topic: Controlling your temper.
Biblical Basis: Proverbs 16

Purpose of this Session:

Every one of us has a temper. It is not uncommon for young people to see it flare in hurtful ways from adults who should have learned better. This TalkSheet will give your kids an opportunity to examine how they react in temper-flaring situations and to discuss what kind of behavior and self-control they can strive for.

To Introduce the Topic:

Set up three corners of the room: one for short-fused people, one for even-tempered people, and one for very easygoing people. Suggest various scenarios, and ask kids to go to the corner that they think would represent how they would handle the pressure to explode in anger. Scenarios you could suggest include: Someone insults you; someone insults your mother; someone beats up your friend; someone beats up your five-year-old brother; someone breaks something and then blames you; someone cusses you out; someone gives you an obscene gesture; someone slanders your race or gender; someone steals from you..

The Discussion:

Item #1: Continue the dialogue you have started by discussing the last time your kids lost their tempers and why. Discuss why they lost their cool. Share a situation where you lost your temper, and why.

Item #2: Talk about the idea of healthy anger. Even Jesus was angry at times. Help your students to recognize the difference between valid anger and temperamental acting out.

Item #3: Point out how much damage can be done when a person blows his or her stack. Ask your kids to share how they react when someone else blows his or her stack.

Item #4: Have kids share their answers. Ask, "Can people control their tempers, or is there a point where everyone loses their ability to control themselves?" Allow for disagreement.

Item #5: Have your kids share which passages seem most important. Discuss how a person can use calmness to cool down a volatile situation, and the potential consequences of being a hot-tempered person.

Item #6: Ask your students to think carefully about how they handled their last temper tantrum. Encourage them to seek that person out and ask for forgiveness for mishandling the situation.

To Close the Session:

Challenge your students to consider if they have wronged someone with their temper. Encourage them to go to that person and seek forgiveness. Remind your students that while they might be correct about what created their anger, they could have been wrong about how they handled their anger.

Outside Activity:

Invite your students to find a partner that they can call if a situation comes up in the next week that provokes them to anger. The job of the partner is to urge self-control, patience, and restraint, as well as being a listening ear.

aNd tHeN He said...

1 **If you had a secret that you wanted to tell one person, who would it be?**

___Best friend   ___Parent   ___Minister   ___Teacher   ___Brother or sister

___Grandparent   ___Coach   ___Stranger   ___Other: _____

2 Have you ever had someone tell others what you told them in confidence?   ___**Yes** ___**No**

If yes, how did it make you feel? _____

How did it change your relationship with that person?_____

_____

3 **For which of the "secrets" below would you break confidence?** (Circle the ones you would reveal.)

Your friend tells you who he is secretly in love with.

Your friend says she is pregnant.

Your friend says she is pregnant and plans to get an abortion.

Your friend confesses he cheated on the English final.

Your friend tells you that he shoplifted.

Your friend tells you that her uncle is sexually abusing her.

Your friend tells you that she is experimenting with drugs.

Your friend tells you she thinks she is homosexual.

Your friend tells you that he is going to run away from home.

Your friend tells you that he is HIV positive.

Your friend tells you that he is thinking of suicide.

4 Read the passages below. Pick out a short phrase that describes the idea behind each verse:

Proverbs 11:13_____

Proverbs 17:9_____

Proverbs 20:19_____

Ephesians 4:29_____

Date Used_____ Group _____

AND THEN HE SAID . . .

Topic: Gossip.
Biblical Basis: Proverbs 17

Purpose of this Session:
Young people often have lots of secrets. As they pull away from their parents, teens find themselves less willing to disclose private thoughts to their parents. Instead, most kids trust other kids with their secrets, often resulting in an information leak. For some kids, nothing is as fun as leaking a juicy tidbit from somebody's life. This is known in the Bible as gossip—the telling of what does not need to be told for the fun of the telling.

Gossip is a national pastime in our culture. Adults, kids, and the media seem to revel in gossip. But while it is fun to hear, gossip is also hurtful. It can destroy reputations and tear apart friendships. This TalkSheet will help kids to discover that only some things need to be shared with others, and that keeping a confidence will strengthen friendships and build trust between people.

To Introduce the Topic:
As your kids come into the room, start whispering about them to other students. From time to time, point and giggle. Whisper that they are to do this (whisper, laugh, and point) to other kids as they arrive. Use this as a fun way to begin the discussion about gossip.

Or buy an edition of a supermarket tabloid, select two or three articles, and bring them to the class with you. Ask your students to vote on which stories they think are true and which they think are false. Discuss what sells those tabloids. Rewrite one of the stories using the names of some of the kids in your group. Talk about what it would feel like to have these kind of stories written about us.

The Discussion:
Item #1: Allow your students to discuss who they would be most likely to trust with a secret. Have a few willing students share why they would trust the person they named.
Item #2: Discuss the feelings that come when a confidence has been violated. Have a few willing students share what happened to them, and what the betrayal by their friends did to their relationship.
Item #3: Go over which secrets a real friend would not keep (e.g., suicide threats, sexual abuse). Then ask kids which other secrets should be revealed. Be prepared for a lot of disagreement on some of these issues.
Item #4: Have a few willing students share their phrases (e.g., being trustworthy, betraying a confidence, promoting love, wholesome talk). Talk to your students about the impact that breaking a confidence has on friendships, trust, and our integrity as Christians.

To Close the Session:
Point out to your students that we human beings are funny creatures. We love the tidbits of scandal, the lure of knowing something that others would rather keep private. Explain that this is our old nature at work, keeping us busy with nonsense or intrigue and focused on anything but the essentials of true Christian living. Address the need to keep watch over what we say and whom we say it to.

Outside Activity:
Help your students create a pin out of old buttons and clasps that each of them can wear to school or churches as a reminder that they are to "Button Their Lips" when it comes to gossip. This can be real fun if all of the kids refuse to tell others what the pins stand for. It will make people crazy and may start a fad, or cause lots of gossip about the button pin itself.

A FRIEND INDEED!

1 Is it easy or hard to make friends?   ____Easy   ____Hard
Is it easy or hard to keep friends for a long time?   ____Easy   ____Hard
Is it easy or hard to break apart a friendship?   ____Easy   ____Hard

2 If you were able to go into a supermarket of "friends" and select qualities off the shelf that are important to a friendship, **which five of the following would you pick?** (Circle only five.)

Similar interests	Loyal	Funny	Smart	Athletic
Keep secrets	Musical	Popular	Truthful	Spiritual
Trustworthy	Honest	Handsome or pretty	Same age	Same race
Wealthy	Outgoing	Christian	Creative	Humble
Easygoing	Witty	Patient	Kind	Generous
Clean	Cheerful	Courageous	Responsible	Industrious

3 **Read the following Bible passages. What does each passage say about what a friend is like?**

Proverbs 17:17 _____

Proverbs 18:24 _____

Proverbs 27:6 _____

Proverbs 27:9-10 _____

4 Which do you think are **true** or **false** about friendship?

a. A friend will never tell you what you don't want to hear.   TRUE___ FALSE___
b. A friend will stick with you no matter what.   TRUE___ FALSE___
c. A friend can be closer to you than a relative.   TRUE___ FALSE___
d. A friend will try to prevent others from making bad choices.   TRUE___ FALSE___
e. Two friends will like the very same things.   TRUE___ FALSE___
f. A friendship can be worn out by too much togetherness.   TRUE___ FALSE___
g. A Christian would be sure to tell their friends about Christ.   TRUE___ FALSE___
h. A Christian should only have Christian friends.   TRUE___ FALSE___

5 If you were to write the words on a tombstone for your best friend, what would you say? What would you want to be said about you by your best friends?

BEST FRIEND

ME

A FRIEND INDEED!

Topic: Friendship.
Biblical Basis: Proverbs 17; 18; 27

Purpose of this Session:
Friendships are paramount in the life of a young person. As friendships become more and more important, kids must learn what creates and sustains valuable and lasting friendships. They must learn what kind of friends to cultivate as well as what kind of friends to avoid. Most importantly, they must learn what kind of friend they need to become. This TalkSheet will help kids to discover that friends can be one of the greatest gifts that God gives them.

To Introduce the Topic:
Give your students paper and pencils. Tell them to draw four columns on their paper. In each column, have them write the following seven headings: Name, Hobbies and Interests, Color, Pets, Entertainment, Sports, Worst Moment. When you say "Go," each student must interview four other students and get all of the information from them including their first, middle, and last names; any hobbies or interests (they must say something); their favorite colors; what pets they have or last had; their favorite movies, TV programs, or bands; any sports they enjoy; and the worst moments in their lives.

Give a prize to the first person to get all four columns completely filled. Have a few willing students read out information about others they discovered. Then talk about how friendships often develop as we discover more about each other.

The Discussion:
Item #1: Talk about the process of making and keeping friends. Discuss what might cause friendships to dissolve and what can make friendships last a long time.
Item #2: Discuss the qualities of a real friend. Explore which are the most desirable to have.
Item #3: Have a few willing students share their answers (e.g., a friend loves at all times, loyalty is important, you can trust a real friend, you don't run out on your friends). Talk about the ideas the Bible contributes to the area of friendship. Discuss why a friend who has to tell you bad news is better than flattery from an enemy, and why friends are important to have for advice and help.
Item #4: Discuss myths and fallacies about friendship. Talk about the need to have both Christian and non-Christian friends as well as our responsibility to share Christ with our nonbelieving friends.
Item #5: Have your kids share what they would say about a friend as a tribute. Discuss the things that make these friendships special.

To Close the Session:
Point out to your students the need to be a friend as well as to accumulate them. Let them know that friendships take work, patience, and wisdom if they are going to last. Tell them about some of the famous friendships in the Bible like David and Jonathan, Jesus and his disciples, and Paul and Timothy. Point out that we should never use our friends, but seek ways to help them out.

Outside Activity:
Ask your kids to attempt to make a new friend this week. They can do this by inviting someone they do not know well to eat lunch with them at school, bring someone to youth group, or another simple activity.

Wise Up

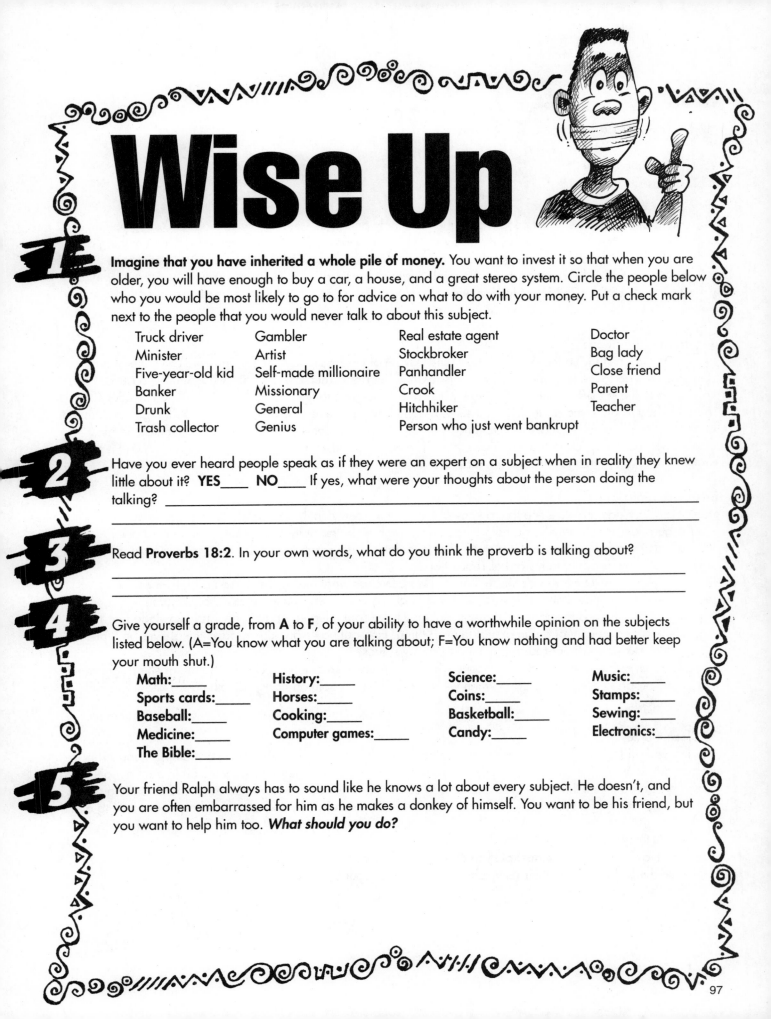

1 **Imagine that you have inherited a whole pile of money.** You want to invest it so that when you are older, you will have enough to buy a car, a house, and a great stereo system. Circle the people below who you would be most likely to go to for advice on what to do with your money. Put a check mark next to the people that you would never talk to about this subject.

Truck driver	Gambler	Real estate agent	Doctor
Minister	Artist	Stockbroker	Bag lady
Five-year-old kid	Self-made millionaire	Panhandler	Close friend
Banker	Missionary	Crook	Parent
Drunk	General	Hitchhiker	Teacher
Trash collector	Genius	Person who just went bankrupt	

2 Have you ever heard people speak as if they were an expert on a subject when in reality they knew little about it? **YES____** **NO____** If yes, what were your thoughts about the person doing the talking? _____
_____

3 Read **Proverbs 18:2**. In your own words, what do you think the proverb is talking about?
_____
_____

4 Give yourself a grade, from **A** to **F**, of your ability to have a worthwhile opinion on the subjects listed below. (A=You know what you are talking about; F=You know nothing and had better keep your mouth shut.)

Math:____	**History:____**	**Science:____**	**Music:____**
Sports cards:____	**Horses:____**	**Coins:____**	**Stamps:____**
Baseball:____	**Cooking:____**	**Basketball:____**	**Sewing:____**
Medicine:____	**Computer games:____**	**Candy:____**	**Electronics:____**
The Bible:____			

5 Your friend Ralph always has to sound like he knows a lot about every subject. He doesn't, and you are often embarrassed for him as he makes a donkey of himself. You want to be his friend, but you want to help him too. ***What should you do?***

WISE UP

Topic: Speaking wisely.
Biblical Basis: Proverbs 18

Purpose of this Session:

Everyone has an opinion. Most people offer them willingly on subjects they know little about. Young people are no exceptions. Often they can be heard loudly stating their ideas on all kinds of things they know nothing about.

Godly wisdom teaches us to seek understanding, insight, and knowledge. It teaches us to listen more than we talk. It is good advice for a generation who thinks that just because we have the ability to express our opinions, we ought to do so. This TalkSheet session will help your students see that while everyone has an opinion, not everyone is entitled to hold an opinion.

To Introduce the Topic:

Have your group stand in the center of the room. Ask all of the kids who think foreign cars are better than domestic cars go to the left, and those who disagree to the right. Then ask all those who think Ford builds better cars to go to the left side of the room, those who prefer Chevrolet to the middle, and those who consider Chrysler to be the best to go to the right. Allow those who don't have a clue to sit down. Try the same thing with different brands of cereal, different makes of clothing, etc. Talk about how some people have an opinion about most everything and are quick to show it. Show that on some things (like which breakfast cereal tastes best) it doesn't matter, but on other things, our opinion may demonstrate our ignorance.

The Discussion:

Item #1: Most kids are wise enough to know the difference between those who deserve to be consulted about a money question and those who do not. Discuss why we hold better opinions of some people than others.
Item #2: Have a few willing students share their examples. Discuss what a person who talks about what he or she doesn't know is doing to his or her reputation.
Item #3: Have a few willing kids share their answers. Discuss what makes the person a fool—the lack of motivation to truly understand a situation in favor of airing one's own opinion about that situation.
Item #4: Ask your kids to share what areas that they have some degree of authority and knowledge in. Talk about why a person cannot be an expert in everything. Find out how your kids graded themselves on Bible knowledge. How does that area rank on their priority scores?
Item #5: Talk about what to say to someone who has the problem of talking about what he or she is ignorant of. Discuss appropriate ways to respond when we are asked for an opinion about something we know little or nothing about.

To Close the Session:

Remind your kids that they will often hear people talking about things they know little or nothing about. This is particularly true when it comes to the Bible. They will hear ideas and opinions about the Bible from people who have never read it. Tell them that God wants us to be people who speak wisely, who seek understanding and information rather than react blindly. He wants us to be the kind of people who know what we are talking about.

Outside Activity:

Ask your kids to become a mini-expert on one subject that interests them during the next week. Have a few willing students share about their new subject of interest at your next meeting.

GOOD REP

1 **Which of the following comes closest to describing what you think your reputation might be?**

___Clown   ___Jock   ___Introvert   ___Bubblehead
___Studious   ___Spiritual   ___Outgoing   ___Shy
___Friendly   ___Humorous   ___Daring   ___Dumb
___Smart   ___Leader   ___Hardworking   ___Mechanical
___Pretty   ___Tasteful   ___Generous   ___Tough
___Cool   ___Hunter   ___Clumsy   ___Brave
___Moody   ___Old-fashioned   ___Progressive   ___Talented

2 Someone once said, *"A good reputation takes a long time to build, but only a moment to destroy."*

Do you: AGREE_____ or DISAGREE_____? Why or why not?_____

_____

3 Read **Proverbs 22:1**. What do you think it means to you? _____

_____

4 Some things can help you have a good reputation, and some can bring a reputation down. Put a plus sign (**+**) next to the items listed below that would give a person a good name, and a minus sign (**−**) next to the items you think would negatively affect a reputation:

___Lying   ___Patient   ___Prejudiced   ___Kind
___Good humor   ___Lazy   ___Generous   ___Gossiper
___Devious   ___Imaginative   ___Helpful   ___Self-controlled
___Righteous   ___Quarrelsome   ___Merciful   ___Bossy
___Self-centered   ___Cautious   ___Caring   ___Humble
___Proud   ___Moral   ___Immoral   ___Boastful
___Peaceful   ___Hardworking   ___Loyal

5 In what ways does a person who has a good reputation benefit from it?

_____
_____
_____

In what ways does a person who has a bad reputation suffer from it?

_____
_____
_____

GOOD REP

Topic: Reputation.
Biblical Basis: Proverbs 22

Purpose of this Session:

Every teen wants to be liked, admired, and accepted. Kids dress for the approval of their peers, act out roles for their applause, and feel great pain when they think they are being rejected. This TalkSheet session deals with a subject that is right where most kids live every day: building a reputation that encourages others to like them.

A good reputation is valuable to any teen. It precedes them, it sets the tone in which they are viewed, and often predetermines the amount of trust and openness they will receive from others. Your students will learn that developing a good reputation takes effort and struggle. But it is worth it.

To Introduce the Topic:

Bring in some newspapers or magazines. Toss them to the group, along with a few pairs of scissors. Ask your kids to cut out advertisements that tie in a product with a person's reputation. Pin what they have cut out on a corkboard. Discuss why reputation would be important to consumers. Remind your kids that people are only as trustworthy as their reputations.

The Discussion:

Item #1: Have your kids select words that might describe the reputation that they think they have with others. Have a few willing students share their answers.

Item #2: Discuss the process of building or dismantling a reputation. Share a time when your reputation suffered, what caused the problem, and what it took to repair your reputation.

Item #3: Talk about the value that the Bible applies to a good name or reputation. Ask how much the price tag would be if a person had to "buy" a good reputation.

Item #4: Explore the various characteristics or habits that would enhance or destroy a reputation. Note that the things that build a good reputation are the things that also fit with godly living.

Item #5: Have a few willing students share their answers. Try to help your kids realize the benefits of a good reputation: being trusted, being someone others come to for help and advice, having the respect of peers, etc.

To Close the Session:

Explain to your students how important it is that we put energy and effort into living lives that will give us a good reputation. Talk about how obeying God will produce a life that a person can be proud of. Ask your students to consider the kind of reputation that they are after, and whether that reputation will end up hurting them in the end. Close by asking your kids to contribute one thought or idea that would be a plus in building a good reputation; for example, "If you want a good name, hang around with good people."

Outside Activity:

Invite each student to select a nickname for a trait that they would like to make part of their personality and reputation. This should be a trait that they desire, but feel they have little of. The names could be out of a name book or simply made up. For example, a person who wants to listen more than they talk can take the nickname "Ears" or "Zipper Mouth." Have your students share their nicknames and commit to addressing one another by their new nicknames for the following week.

DOLLARS WITH WINGS

1 **If you had three wishes that could come true, would one of them be to have lots of money?**
___Naturally   ___I don't think so   ___I dunno!

2 What is the largest amount of your own money you have ever spent at one time? _____
What did you spend it on? _____ Would you do it again?_____
Why or why not?_____

3 **What do you think is the biggest danger in desiring to make lots of money?** List them in order, with the greatest danger being number 1, and the least danger being number 6:

___ *Doing dishonest things to get it*
___ *Ignoring other priorities to make money*
___ *Worshipping money more than God*
___ *Thinking you don't need to depend on God anymore*
___ *Getting lots of money but no happiness*
___ *Using people for what you could get from them rather than caring about them for who they are*

4 Read **Proverbs 23:4-5**. Draw a picture in the space below of what you feel this passage is talking about:

Now read about the rich man in **Luke 12:15-21**. Fill in the blanks to the passage below:
Jesus said to be on guard against all kinds of _____ and that a person's life does not consist in the abundance of _____ In his parable, he told of a rich man whose _____ produced a huge crop. His problem was that he didn't have enough _____ for his crop. He decided to build bigger _____ and to "take life easy: _____, _____ and be _____". But God had a different idea. He said to him, "This very night your_____ will be demanded from you." God even called him a _____. Jesus commented that this is how it will be for anyone who is not _____ toward God.

5 **What do these two passages tell you about the desire to get rich?**

6 **Where is the desire to make lots of money on your scale of important things?** Mark your answer below:

|_____|_____|_____|_____|_____|_____|_____|_____|_____|_____|
Highest priority   **Lowest priority**

Date Used_____ Group _____

DOLLARS WITH WINGS

Topic: The desire for wealth.
Biblical Basis: Proverbs 23

Purpose of this Session:

High schoolers are at the age where money talks! Many kids have bought into the idea that happiness and money are directly related. Some of your kids may already be forming the habits and worldview that will cause them misery throughout their adult lives as they chase after the elusive pot of gold.

The Bible is cold to the topic of striving for wealth. It warns kids and adults alike that the minute they fix their gaze upon the dollar, it sprouts wings and flies away like an elusive butterfly. This TalkSheet session is designed to help your kids see that material gain is the wrong place to put their focus, and that real eternal treasure is made up of things that don't disappear.

To Introduce the Topic:

Divide your room into two sections. Mark one section with a sign that says, "The Pay is Great;" the other section, with a sign that says, "The Work is Enjoyable." Tell your students that they must choose a career. One job pays $100,000 per year but is really boring. The other job is really fun, but pays barely enough to get by. Ask your students to select the job they would choose for a career, and to go to the sign that reflects their choice. After they have chosen, discuss the reasons for their choices. Use this discussion as an opportunity to introduce today's topic.

The Discussion:

Item #1: Use this question to further the discussion of our desire for money. Ask, "Why does money appear on so many of our wish lists?"

Item #2: Have a few willing students share their answers. See if any of your kids have regrets about money they have spent in the past. Talk about the tendency to burn with desire for some object, only to become bored with it once we have acquired it.

Item #3: Talk about the problems that money creates in our spiritual lives. See which difficulties seem most dangerous to your students. Also, see if some kids see no danger to acquiring money. Allow for disagreement.

Item #4: Help your kids to create images that illustrate the illusory nature of wealth, especially those students who are not artists. Encourage a few kids to share their drawings, and affirm them profusely.

Item #5: Talk about where the priorities and desires of Christians should be focused. Discuss how a person builds up treasure in heaven.

Item #6: Allow your students to determine where the desire to get money sits on their priority list. See if your students can come up with a place on the graph where warning lights should go on.

To Close the Session:

Since the desire to surround ourselves with things and the urge to grasp after money is so universal, we must constantly keep on guard that we do not come under its spell. Encourage your students to make it the goal of their lives to invest in things that cannot be taken away from them.

Outside Activity:

Challenge your students to do something for a person in your church who does not have the means to repay the deed. Your kids could wash cars, mow lawns, make meals, watch the kids of weary or sick parents, etc.

A REAL LIFESAVER

1   **Would you risk your life to save:**

A baby	___Yes	___No
An old person	___Yes	___No
A criminal	___Yes	___No
A dog	___Yes	___No
A friend	___Yes	___No
A person with AIDS	___Yes	___No
A family member	___Yes	___No
A cult leader	___Yes	___No

2   Do you agree or disagree with the following statement: "People who need spiritual help should be responded to with the same urgency as people who need physical help."

AGREE_____   **DISAGREE_____**

WHY OR WHY NOT?_____

_____

3   Read Proverbs 24:11-12. Then, answer the following questions:

Who is this passage directed to?_____

Who is it talking about? _____

What is their problem? _____

What should we do about it? _____

How might we try to avoid our responsibility? _____

How could our actions be judged? _____

4   **HOW** might a person be led to spiritual death? **WHO** might be leading them? **WHAT** activities might contribute towards a person's spiritual destruction?

_____

_____

5   Suppose you wanted to try and rescue some of your friends from dying spiritually. List, in order of effectiveness, **which ways would be the best to conduct the rescue**, with number one being the most effective:

___Mail them a letter about Christ	___Bring them to a church service	___Give them a Bible
___Send the minister over to talk to them	___Act spiritual around them	___Give them tract
___Preach a sermon to them	___Tell them what Christ means to you	___Pray for them
___Loan them a Christian CD	___Bring them to youth group	

6   What are some excuses that kids might come up with for not trying to rescue their friends from a sure spiritual death? _____   _____

_____   _____

_____   _____

Date Used_____ Group_____

A REAL LIFESAVER

Topic: Sharing Christ.
Biblical Basis: Proverbs 24

Purpose of this Session:
The commission to tell others the Good News of Jesus Christ has no age boundaries. High schoolers rub shoulders daily with those who are being led away to spiritual death by a river of false ideas flowing from a secular world. Christians are called to the rescue. Because of their proximity, kids have the initial responsibility to rescue other kids. They are closest to the scene and are trusted by their friends.

The obligation to gently but boldly share Christ with their friends is scary to most kids. They have a million reasons why they can't do it. Often this is because they think that they must give a well-defined doctrinal presentation.

This TalkSheet session is designed to not only prod kids to consider reaching out to their non-Christian friends, but to let them know that there is an effective and easy way to do it: Share about what Jesus Christ means to them personally, in their own words, and their own ways.

To Introduce the Topic:
Invite willing students to talk about a recent accident they might have seen or driven by. Talk about what happened. Who was first at the scene? What actions did they take? What was the response of other bystanders? Discuss what, if anything, the student telling the story did to help. Talk about what might have happened if there was no one around when this accident took place. Use this as an opportunity to present the idea that people can be in dire need, and that even kids can do something to help.

The Discussion:
Item #1: Have kids share who they might be motivated to risk their life to save. Many kids will likely identify a friend as one of those people. Point out that most people would risk a lot to save one of their friends.
Item #2: Allow for some disagreement here. Help your kids to define what spiritual needs are—that kids' very souls are in jeopardy without God.
Item #3: Be prepared for some strong reactions to this passage. It will be hard for some kids to face their responsibilities. Also, some kids will dispute that people really end up in hell.
Item #4: Help kids to understand how the everyday, unhealthy activities that any of us can fall into—obsession with money, sexual temptation, etc.—can actually lead to spiritual death.
Item #5: Discuss which method of telling others about Christ is the most effective. Let your kids brainstorm on this. Ask your students what would have the most effect upon them?
Item #6: Have a few willing students share their answers. Help kids to see that it's usually our fear that keeps us from reaching out to our friends. Point out that they don't have to be theological experts; they just have to share what God has done for them, in their own words.

To Close the Session:
Explain to your group that though it can be hard to understand, many people are in danger of being led to eternal death. Read Ephesians 2:1-5; point out that spiritual death is the result of not knowing Christ personally.

Outside Activity:
Challenge your kids to think of at least one person that they will attempt to share Christ with in some way during the next week. Have them report on the results of their efforts at your next meeting.

How to treat an ENEMY

 1 Can you think of anyone who you would consider an **ENEMY?** Put that person's initials here:_____

 2 Circle the ways that people normally relate to their enemies:

Put them down whenever possible   Help them out if they are needed
Send them Christmas cards   Think about ways to torture them
Talk to them on the phone   Dislike their friends and family too
Give them dirty looks   Seek vengeance
Have them over for dinner   Look for ways to bless them
Talk to them kindly   Smile at them
Pray for them   Hope they die a slow and painful death

3 Read **Proverbs 25:21-22**; **Matthew 5:43-48**; and **Romans 12:14**. What specific instructions do these passages give in how we should treat our enemies?

 4 Write down three things that your enemy might do or say if you treated him or her like Christ commanded:

_____
_____
_____

 5 If treating our enemies as the way Jesus commanded is the goal for Christians, how successful are you in reaching that goal? Mark your position on the line below.

|____|____|____|____|____|____|____|____|

Fail miserably   **Always like Jesus**

HOW TO TREAT AN ENEMY

Topic: Loving our enemies.
Biblical Basis: Proverbs 25

Purpose of this Session:

Christ's teaching on how to relate to enemies is so contrary to our nature that teens are sure to pull back in surprise at the essence of this session. They have learned to deal with enemies in a manner far different than that required by Jesus. Vengeance and revenge is what they are used to; benevolence and kindness seem bizarre by comparison.

But God knows that the delight of feeding on hatred soon does more damage to the human soul than any enemy could inflict. He seeks to win the enemy over rather than annihilate them.

Most kids will struggle with the plan God lays out. They cannot imagine that it would do anything more than put them in a position of weakness. This TalkSheet session provides a great opportunity to challenge students to see if they really trust God enough to follow his commands, even when they seem crazy.

To Introduce the Topic:

Draw up a list of twenty feuding pairs, both real and fictional (e.g., The Road Runner vs. Wile E. Coyote; Darth Vader vs. Luke Skywalker; General Grant vs. General Lee; Tweety Bird vs. Sylvester the Cat; Yitzhak Rabin vs. Yasser Arafat). Use this list to hold a fun contest with your kids.

Pass out papers and pencils to your kids with one-half of the adversary pairs listed. Your kids' task is to fill in the second half of the list with the correct adversary. Give small prizes to those who get the most correct pairs.

The Discussion:

Item #1: Discuss who in your group has enemies. Ask them, "What makes someone an enemy?"
Item #2: Talk about the way people treat those who they think of as enemies. Ask, "Which of the ways listed seem totally crazy? Why?"
Item #3: Ask your students to describe the treatment that Scripture says we must give to our enemies. Discuss how this conflicts with the way people usually treat those they dislike.
Item #4: Have a few willing students share their answers. Many of them will say things like, "They'd think I was crazy!" Then ask, "How would you react if your enemy treated you as Christ commanded?"
Item #5: Talk about why loving your enemies is a tall order for most people. Allow your students to privately evaluate where they are in their ability to practice what the Bible teaches on this subject.

To Close the Session:

Explain to your group that it is difficult, but not impossible, to care for those who hate us. Let them know that this process is done one step at a time, starting with something simple such as refusing to say bad things about the person. Once they've succeeded at little things, they can go on to other gestures of goodwill. Point out that we are not told to act kindly only if the other person responds, but whether they respond positively or not.

Outside Activity:

Have your kids rewrite Matthew 5:43-48 by substituting the name of a person who they would consider their enemy for the word "enemy." Ask your kids to take their rewrite home and place it where they can be reminded about how God wants them to treat that person.

'fess up

1 **Do you think it is easy or hard to conceal wrongdoing?**
____Easy   ____Hard
Why?

2 **What are the top five reasons people cover up what they do wrong?** Mark them in order, with one being the top reason:

___ They are afraid that others will think they are weird.
___ They are ashamed of what they did.
___ They are afraid of what their parents will say.
___ They think others will feel they are a hypocrite.
___ They are afraid of punishment.
___ They don't want to be humiliated in public.
___ They are afraid they will get a police record.
___ They are afraid they will get a bad reputation.
___ They will have to stop doing what they are doing.
___ It is more fun if no one knows about it.

3 Edward was caught shoplifting at a neighborhood store. As part of his punishment, Edward's parents made him go to the manager and each person who worked in the store and say to them, "I am a thief. I have stolen things from your store. I am sorry and I will pay you for the things I took."

Do you think the punishment was (check one):

a. ___Fair and just   d. ___A sure way to cure shoplifting
b. ___Too harsh   e. ___Child abuse
c. ___Too embarrassing   f. ___Stupid and ineffective

4 Read **Proverbs 28:13; Isaiah 29:15;** and **1 John 1:9**. Then complete the following sentences:
It is a bad idea to try to hide _____. It is futile anyhow because God always
_____. Better to _____ our sins because then we will find
_____.

5 Should we ever confess our wrongdoing to another person?
____**Yes**   ____**No**
If yes, to who? _____
Why? _____

6 **If you wanted to confess wrongdoing to another person, who would you go to?**
___Pastor or youth worker   ___Relative
___Parent   ___Schoolteacher or coach
___Adult friend   ___Other

'FESS UP

Topic: Confessing our sins.
Biblical Basis: Proverbs 28

Purpose of this Session:
Kids, like most human beings, find it difficult to confess when they have done wrong. Sin stays buried, haunting and putrefying the soul.

The Bible urges confession. It is a healthy cleansing process, the beginning of mercy and forgiveness. It breeds humility, for there is no reality check like admitting our failures.

This TalkSheet session will encourage your kids to be honest about their spiritual failures. Your kids will be challenged to quickly admit their sins to God and to find a trusted person to confide in.

To Introduce the Topic:
Play a little game of Truth or Dare with your students. Prepare, or have your students help prepare, a list of questions to answer if they choose truth and penalties to pay if they choose dare. At random, pick students who must answer the question truthfully. If they refuse to answer, they must pay the penalty. For example, a question might be, "Who is your secret love?" A student who doesn't want to reveal that information must pay a penalty such as "Do five pushups." If your students help make the questions and penalties, reserve the right to edit them. After you play for awhile, talk a bit about the kind of things people were hesitant to reveal.

The Discussion:
Item #1: Have your students talk about which is easier and braver: to hide or to conceal wrongdoing. Point out that the cowardly act is to conceal wrongdoing.
Item #2: Discuss the reasons that people tend to cover up wrongdoing. See if there are any patterns to your students' answers. Share an incident where you covered up a wrongdoing, why you covered it up, and what resulted from your actions.
Item #3: Have a few willing students share their answers. Ask, "Was Edward's confession valid since it was forced? How effective do you think his punishment was? Will it keep Edward from stealing again?"
Item #4: Explore the teaching of the Bible on confession of sin and the futility of concealment. Discuss the all-knowing power of God and his desire to forgive and have mercy.
Item #5: Most kids will have no problem confessing to God. Talk about when and if we should confess our sins to another person, and even ask for forgiveness from them. This is where it can get sticky—but don't let your kids off the hook.
Item #6: Talk about who would be a trusted confessor to your kids. Ask, "What qualities would you look for in a confidant?"

To Close the Session:
Since God lovingly offers forgiveness and mercy to those who learn the habit of confessing, it is to your kids' advantage to begin to practice the art of confession. Distribute paper and pencils, then ask your students to write out a confession to God about something that they have done wrong. Invite any willing kids who are brave enough to make a public confession of their sins as well.

Outside Activity:
Explore designing a peer counseling program with your kids. There are several good books designed to help set this kind of program up, including *Peer Counseling In Youth Groups* and *Advanced Peer Counseling in Youth Groups* by Joan Sturkie and Dr. Siang-Yan Tan (Youth Specialties/Zondervan).

WORDS TO LIVE BY

1 Which do you think is TRUE?

___ *The Bible could be God's Word.*

___ *The Bible is an old book of myths and fables, but not God's Word.*

___ *The Bible has some of God's words in it.*

___ *The Bible is God's Word.*

2 **When people read the Bible, they should** (check which you think is true):

___ Believe and follow only what their heart tells them to.

___ Believe and follow only what their church or minister tells them to.

___ Study carefully, then obey what is clearly taught.

___ See it as a suggestion list rather than strict guidelines.

___ Enjoy it as literature.

3 Many religions have their own holy books. Some groups have added to, or taken away from, what is found in the Bible. **What would you say** to one of these people if they insisted that they had a new and improved version of God's Word? _____

_____

4 Read the following passages, then select one word for each that best describes the **attributes of God's Word:**

Proverbs 30:5 _____

2 Timothy 3:15-16 _____

Hebrews 4:12 _____

Luke 11:28 _____

5 Why do some people who trust the Bible as God's Word fail to spend much time reading it?

_____

_____

6 Which is true for you? (Check one.)

___**I read the Bible a lot.**

___**I need to read the Bible more.**

___**I am comfortable with how much I read the Bible.**

___**I read the Bible, but don't obey much of what it says.**

WORDS TO LIVE BY

Topic: The divinity of the Bible.
Biblical Basis: Proverbs 30

Purpose of this Session:

The writer of Proverbs tells us that every word of God is flawless. Indeed, all the wisdom humans can muster is only a flicker of light compared to the incredible illumination that comes from the pages of the Bible.

For some kids, years spent in Sunday school has dulled the wonder of this truth. This TalkSheet session is designed to reemphasize the fact that the Bible is God's unique Word to humankind. Kids will discover that God provides us with a refuge, a rule of instruction for living life, a love letter, and an instrument for touching the most private parts of our lives—all packaged in pages of paper and ink.

To Introduce the Topic:

Bring in an instruction book for any device, from a computer to a VCR. Find out how many of your kids tend to read instruction books and how many tend to avoid them or only read them when they are stuck. Talk about how we can foul up our purchases when we fail to follow the instruction manuals. Compare this with the Bible—God's instruction manual for human beings.

The Discussion:

Item # 1: Discuss the various viewpoints on the authority of the Bible. Allow for disagreement on this. Be prepared to explain what makes the Bible unique and accurate.

Item #2: Have a few willing students share their responses. Find out how much diversity you have in views toward Scripture in your group.

Item #3: Help your kids to see how they can respond to those who also claim they have God's word. Point out that the Bible has survived innumerable attacks, alterations, and other abuses and still powerfully testifies to a risen Christ.

Item #4: Discuss what the Bible says about itself. Point out how this information relates to the previous questions.

Item #5: Talk about why people who say they believe the Bible is God's word do not spend much time reading it—laziness, a feeling that it's hard to understand, fear of seeing challenging commands from God, etc. Have a few willing students share why they may have trouble spending time in the Bible, and, if accurate, share your struggles with regular Bible reading.

Item #6: Ask your students to evaluate how seriously they take the Bible to be God's word. Talk about ways to make the Bible easier to access for kids—topical Bible discussions, devotional guides, etc.

To Close the Session:

Explain to your group the need to spend adequate time in the Word of God. Go over with your kids at least one devotional plan that they could implement during the week. Ask each of your students to pledge to spend a specific time reading the Bible daily this week.

Outside Activity:

Invite a resource person to speak to your group about the evidence for the Bible and the reliability of Scripture. Make sure to emphasize to your speaker the age level they should prepare for. Allow kids to prepare questions in advance for this resource person.

A Woman's Place

1 **Which roles do you think women can fulfill?** Circle those and cross out any roles that you think women cannot fulfill.

Cook	Soldier	Weightlifter	Salesperson	Farmer
Pro football player	Bookkeeper	Pastor	Police officer	Counselor
Wife	Manager	Dentist	President	Truck driver
Scientist	Stockbroker	Surgeon	Firefighter	Businessperson
Construction worker	Mother	Seamstress		

2 How should the roles of wives and husbands be balanced? Mark your answers on the chart below:
Who should do the following most or all of the time?

•Cook the meals	___Wife ___Husband	___50/50	___Whoever is the best cook
•Raise the kids	___Wife ___Husband	___50/50	___Nanny
•Clean the house	___Wife ___Husband	___50/50	___Maid
•Service the car	___Wife ___Husband	___50/50	___The better mechanic
•Check suspicious noises	___Wife ___Husband	___50/50	___Dog
•Wash the clothes	___Wife ___Husband	___50/50	___Send it out
•Make most of the money	___Wife ___Husband	___50/50	___Win lottery
•Buy gifts and flowers	___Wife ___Husband	___50/50	___100/100
•Oversee finances	___Wife ___Husband	___50/50	___E.F. Hutton
•Discipline the kids	___Wife ___Husband	___50/50	___Police
•Mow the lawn	___Wife ___Husband	___50/50	___Kid down the street
•Be the spiritual leader	___Wife ___Husband	___50/50	___Anyone!
•Make the bed	___Wife ___Husband	___50/50	___Leave it

3 Read **Proverbs 31:10-31**. In your own words write short phrases for all of the positive things mentioned about this woman:

4 **AGREE** or **DISAGREE** with the following statements:
This woman had a great amount of liberty, and also clearly loved and honored her husband and family.
AGREE ____   **DISAGREE** ____
Why?

This proverb celebrates the abilities of women.
AGREE ____   **DISAGREE** ____
Why?

This passage is proof that the Bible is anti-woman and chauvinistic.
AGREE ____   **DISAGREE** ____
Why?

5 If you are a young woman, what does the description of the woman in Proverbs 31 mean to you?

If you are a young man, what does the description of the woman in Proverbs 31 tell you about women?

A WOMAN'S PLACE

Topic: God affirms women.
Biblical Basis: Proverbs 31

Purpose of this Session:
Gender confusion reigns in our day. Voices from one side call for women to strive for equality; other voices call for a return to old-time roles; still others emphasize difference and equality at the same time. Along the way, the Bible has been swept into the dustbin of outdated ideology by many people. But Scripture speaks of women in glowing and sensible terms.

This TalkSheet session will give your kids a glimpse of what God thinks about women and their abilities. Proverbs 31 describes a woman who loved, supported and cared for her husband and children while she actively participated in business and management. Her actions earned her the praise and respect of all. This balance is what most young women (and men) seek. It is welcome news to kids confused as to how to understand themselves as men and women.

To Introduce the Topic:
Divide your room into agree and disagree sides. Ask your students to move to the side of the room that reflects their feelings about the following statements as you read them one by one:

- If a couple could only have one child, most would rather have a boy than a girl.
- Women have it easier in life.
- I think it is dumb when people refer to God as "She."
- Women should quit work when they want a family.

You will no doubt notice disagreement among your students. Take this opportunity to tell your kids that this session will give them a clearer idea on how God views women and their roles in society.

The Discussion:
Item #1: Talk about the roles that women have in our culture. Discuss why some roles may or may not be suitable for the typical woman. Talk about which role restrictions seem to be based on common sense, and which seem to be based on cultural traditions.
Item #2: Allow for disagreement (and laughter!) on this exercise. Challenge your kids to find biblical support for their positions.
Item #3: Have volunteers share what they came up with. Ask, "Are there some traits that you feel are the most desirable?" See if there are any patterns.
Item #4: Ask, "What does this proverb bring out about the abilities and roles of women?" Discuss how people sometimes represent Christianity as being hostile towards women. [Note: Some of your students may still believe this to be true. Allow for debate on this point, and be prepared to further study the biblical view of women and gender with your students.]
Item #5: Invite both guys and girls to give feedback on what this proverb means to them. Compare the results.

To Close The Session:
Point out that God does not "put the lid" on people because of their gender. Note the balance and industry that this woman had in her life and the respect and love given by her husband and family. Emphasize that Scripture, unlike our culture which can swing to extremes, advocates a balanced, healthy, and servant-oriented outlook on gender and relationships in general.

Outside Activity:
Have each student write what characteristics he or she considers most important for an ideal mate. Keep them anonymous, but have each student mark their paper with an "M" or an "F" according to their gender. When everyone is finished, collect them and list what each gender has said about what they look for in the opposite sex. If you wish, you can separate the guys and girls for this experiment and have a female leader help interpret what the girls have written for the boys and a male leader do the same for the girls.